The
Brown Decision,
Jim Crow,
and
Southern Identity

The
Brown Decision,
Jim Crow,
and
Southern Identity

JAMES C. COBB

Mercer University Lamar Memorial Lectures
No. 48

The University of Georgia Press
Athens and London

© 2005 by The University of Georgia Press
Athens, Georgia 30602
All rights reserved
Set in Cycles by G & S Typesetters, Inc.
Printed and bound by Maple-Vail
The paper in this book meets the guidelines for permanence
and durability of the Committee on Production Guidelines
for Book Longevity of the Council on Library Resources.

Printed in the United States of America
09   08   07   06   05   C   5   4   3   2   1

Library of Congress Cataloging-in-Publication Data
Cobb, James C. (James Charles), 1947–
The Brown decision, Jim Crow, and Southern identity / James C.
Cobb.
      p.   cm. — (Mercer University Lamar Memorial Lectures ;
no. 48)
   Includes bibliographical references (p.) and index.
ISBN-13: 978-0-8203-2498-2 (hardcover : alk. paper)
ISBN-10: 0-8203-2498-1 (hardcover : alk. paper)
1. Brown, Oliver, 1918– — Trials, litigation, etc.   2. Topeka (Kan.).
Board of Education—Trials, litigation, etc.   3. Segregation in
education—Law and legislation—United States.   4. Race dis-
crimination—Law and legislation—United States.   5. African
Americans—Segregation—Southern States—History—20th
century.   6. African Americans—Civil rights—Southern States—
History—20th century.   7. African Americans—Race identity.
8. African Americans—Ethnic identity.   9. Southern States—Race
relations.   I. Title.   II. Lamar memorial lectures ; no. 48
KF4155.C63   2005
344.73'0798—dc22   2005017467

British Library Cataloging-in-Publication Data available

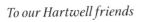

To our Hartwell friends

Contents

Acknowledgments

When I informed Michael Cass that the combination of my duties as chair of the History Department at the University of Georgia and my responsibilities as president of the Southern Historical Association required me to withdraw from the special millennium session of the Dolly Blount Lamar Lectures in October 2000, I feared that my name would be summarily stricken from the esteemed roster of potential future speakers. For once in a very long while, however, my fears went unrealized, and for that I will always be grateful to the Lamar Lectures Committee.

I want to thank Dr. Tony Badger of Cambridge University, Dr. David Garrow of Emory University, and Dr. Robert Haws of the University of Mississippi for sharing their thoughts and suggestions with me as I prepared the lectures. I am especially indebted to Sarah Gardner, who served as our principal host and made our stay in Macon and time at Mercer a supremely pleasant experience. I am also very appreciative of the students who turned out for my talks in truly impressive numbers and gave no sign of having been physically or emotionally coerced to do so. My conversations with Mercer students after the lectures, in classes, and on campus were the high points of my visit. Alumni and friends of Mercer University have good reason to be extremely proud, both of the type of young person their school is attracting and of the job its faculty is doing in developing the students' minds and character.

I made many new friends at Mercer, but I also saw some old ones there as well. My former teachers, colleagues, and longtime friends Will Holmes and Lester Stephens were kind enough to put in an appearance, and my friend and fellow UGA alumnus Glenn Eskew also showed up, accompanied by my mentor and soul mate, Bud

Bartley, whose sudden death a few months later left a hole in my heart that will never heal. My own former students Craig Pascoe and Stephen Taylor turned out to see if the old man could still cut the mustard, or at least spread it around.

No sight warmed my heart during the lectures more than the faces of Cheri Griggs, Nancy and Scott Hardigree, Mary and Allen Jackson, Jean and Billy Kidd, and Joanne Ridgway, all from my hometown of Hartwell, Georgia. Greater love hath no one than he or she who makes a six-hour round-trip to hear me talk, unless it is the love that I feel for them, not only for trekking to Macon but for all the other wonderfully generous and supportive things they have done for us since Lyra and I returned to Hart County in 1997. In a wholly inadequate effort to demonstrate how much these folks mean to us, I am dedicating this book to our dear friends from Hartwell.

The
Brown Decision,
Jim Crow,
and
Southern Identity

Introduction

When I learned that I would be delivering the Lamar Lectures in 2004, I thought immediately of the fiftieth anniversary of the *Brown v. Board of Education* decision. Shortly after that, of course, it occurred to me that I was probably not the only historian who had made this connection and that doubtless a slew of books and anthologies were already in the works and slated for publication in 2004. This meant that by the time my lectures were in print, the scholarly community and the reading public would have been awash in discussions of this topic for at least a year. However, as some of these half-century assessments of *Brown* began to appear as books and articles, I was struck by their general negativity and dismissiveness toward the accomplishments of both the *Brown* decision and, for that matter, the entire civil rights movement. Having made it a lifelong habit to check the wind direction and then run directly against it, I concluded that in order to remain true to form, I should remind folks of what the *Brown* court and the activists who took the spirit of its ruling into the streets were up against, both historically and contemporaneously.

I chose to do this at least in part, I am sure, because as a well-traveled southerner and southern historian now returned to the little town where I grew up, I am continually struck by the magnitude of the changes in racial interaction that have occurred since I was coming along during the last decade and a half of Jim Crow.

As a very young boy in the early 1950s I saw black children, only a little older than I was, trudging up the road in all kinds of weather to Colored Zion School, a two-room structure about a mile away. On several occasions I asked my mama why they didn't ride a bus like the one that carried white kids right past our house (and Colored

Zion School), and her flustered assurances that the black children really didn't mind and probably even preferred it that way left even a naive little boy no more convinced than, I now realize, she was. Later in my childhood, after saying "Yes, sir" or "Yes, ma'am" to black adults or drinking from the same dipper as my black playmates, I received the rebukes that were part of the indoctrination in the rituals of caste that practically every southern child of that era, black or white, was expected to learn and take to heart. As a teenager, I got my first lesson in the economics of discrimination when, after an extremely arduous seven-hour "afternoon" of helping one of my father's friends get up some hay, he asked if I was willing to accept the same pay that he gave Boston Gaines, a black man who worked for him on a regular basis. After agreeing readily, I received the princely sum of $2.50, which was half of what he paid Boston for a twelve-hour day.

Though I did not always comprehend it fully at the time, in my youth I saw countless, sometimes brutal, demonstrations that, in the Jim Crow South, the content of an individual's character or personality counted for little or nothing compared to the color of his or her skin. The memory of some of these incidents makes me cringe even today, and I know that, at the time, they contributed to the steady accretion of doubts about the way whites both regarded and treated African Americans. Still, these doubts remained largely submerged until 1964, which, in a much less dramatic and certainly not the least bit heroic way, became a sort of personal "freedom summer" for me. That June and July I attended Georgia's very first Governor's Honors Program for gifted high school students at Wesleyan College in Macon. Not only was this my first extended stay away from home, but except for one high school English class, it was my first real excursion beyond the parroted verities of my textbooks into the real world of ideas.

It was also my first experience with black classmates of any sort, much less extremely bright and confident ones who had been raised in homes far more affluent than my own. Not only was I suddenly among whites, both students and faculty, who favored integration, but I was actually in an integrated setting with black kids who were clearly my intellectual equals and a lot more. It was an especially tense time; Congress had just passed the Civil Rights Act over the strident objections of an overwhelming majority of southerners in both houses. Meanwhile, murder and mayhem reigned, not just in Philadelphia, Mississippi, but right in my own backyard. In July, Lemuel Penn, a black reservist returning to Washington, D.C., from duty at Fort Benning, was shot and killed crossing the Broad River near Bowman, no more than fifteen miles from our house.

I would like to say that I returned to Hart County High School that fall a tireless crusader for civil rights, but I did not. I was troubled by the growing realization that the social system that shaped the first seventeen years of my life had been dreadfully wrong and extremely hurtful, however unevenly, to all involved. Still, I was either not troubled enough or simply not courageous enough to challenge my elders or my peers, some of whom were clearly incredulous that I had not simply turned around and come home immediately when I discovered that some of my summer classmates in Macon would be black. I did speak out occasionally against the futility of continuing resistance to integration, which did not come to my high school until the fall of 1965. I had completed my entirely segregated twelve years of public education the previous May, precisely eleven Mays after the first *Brown* decision.

Like many white liberals in the mid-twentieth-century South, I was unable to challenge the racial mores of the community in which I was raised until I left it physically. Even then, although the campus environment at the University of Georgia was far more liberal overall, I found that praising the Reverend Martin Luther King Jr. or criticizing George Wallace could still get a fellow student in my face in a hurry. Why I expected more from white kids my age from hometowns much like my own, I don't know, but I did notice that the racial liberalism of most of my professors did not seem to rub off very readily on most of their charges.

However, only after I headed off to teach U.S. history, world history, geography, and English at a recently integrated high school on the outskirts of Atlanta did I begin to fathom either the depth or the breadth of the damage that the Jim Crow system had inflicted. I found noticeable differences in the preparation levels of black and white students of clearly equal ability, as well as a simmering animosity and distrust that could boil over at the slightest provocation, deliberate or otherwise. In fact, shortly after I left my teaching post for military duty, a violent racial incident erupted at the school where my efforts to gain the trust of my black students had at times made me suspect among my white ones as well.

For all that I found wrong with the authoritarian aspects of military life, it presented me with the most racially integrated and egalitarian environment that I'd ever experienced. At the same time, while stationed in New Jersey I quickly learned that color prejudice was by no means contained below the Mason-Dixon line. Perhaps the biggest jolt came when my landlord, a transplanted Frenchman who served as the maitre d' at an exclusive New York restaurant, told me how much he admired white southerners for knowing how to deal with "zee niggers."

Since ascending into the professoriate, I have devoted a great deal of time to studying race relations in the South from a historical perspective, but over the course of my thirty years in academe, I've also tried to keep an eye on the evolving contemporary scene. I am generally numbered among those historians who see more continuity than change in the southern experience, but as someone who knew the South before the Jim Crow system was dismantled, I sometimes think that evidence of the limits of racial change in the region receives more weight than evidence of its extent.

To this end, I have begun this book by examining the way that our historical understanding of segregation evolved in the first half-century after the *Brown* decision. Those who now see the

Jim Crow system as a social anachronism already tottering on the brink of collapse before the *Brown* decree came down are resurrecting a fairly threadbare model that places racial discrimination at odds with economic modernization, when in fact Jim Crow was an integral element of southern development strategy from the end of Reconstruction until the beginning of the civil rights movement. Although the South moved from farm to factory, segregation remained fundamentally intact until, in the wake of *Brown,* civil rights activists succeeded in making segregation a source of the very conflict that it was supposed to prevent.

The second chapter focuses on the arguments of those who feel that the *Brown* decision's contribution to civil rights progress was ultimately less significant than its role in energizing white resistance to it. These revisionist critics, I suggest, have overstated the extent of racial change in the South before *Brown* and understated the decision's role in inspiring and legitimizing the protests that actually played the key role in taking Jim Crow down.

The final chapter argues that the *Brown* decree and the ensuing civil rights movement accomplished not only more than certain compulsively critical pundits are willing to acknowledge but more than even hard statistical evidence of black progress can reveal. The destruction of the Jim Crow system with its "denial of belonging" allowed African Americans both to embrace their identity as southerners and to explore the relationship between their southernness and their blackness. Still, continuing conflict about the Confederate flag and other historical symbols, monuments, and memorials suggests that before blacks and whites can hope to construct a shared vision of southernness, much less a tangible future that both can embrace, they must first come to terms with their differences about a common past they can neither deny nor escape.

As a white southerner from the last generation to grow up under Jim Crow, I am sensitive to the danger of sounding either self-congratulatory or South-congratulatory, especially since I managed to reach adulthood before offering anything more than a tentative critique of a system that I had long since realized was terribly harmful and unjust. On the other hand, however, I believe it would be both a severe distortion of the historical significance of the *Brown* decision and a tragic disservice to those who risked and sacrificed so much to make its spirit a reality in American life to lose sight either of the challenge they faced or the hard-won legacy of their courage and determination.

1 Stranger Than We Thought

Shifting Perspectives on Jim Crow's Career

Writing in 1958, with the outcome of the Little Rock school integration crisis still hanging in the balance and the reenergized post–World War II crusade to recruit new industry to the South going great guns, Oberlin College sociologists George E. Simpson and Milton E. Yinger suggested that segregation could never "survive" in an "industrial society." The current unpleasantness down in Arkansas notwithstanding, "once a society has taken the road of industrialization," they advised, "a whole series of changes begin to take place that undermine the foundation of the segregation system." Two years later economist William H. Nicholls agreed that segregation and industrialization were mutually exclusive, but where Simpson and Yinger believed that the latter would win out, Nicholls argued that the South's entrenched culture of racial discrimination could actually retard industrial expansion in the region. Therefore, Nicholls believed, white southerners must choose between "progress" and "tradition," because "the South can persist in its socially irresponsible doctrine of racism only at the ultimate cost of tearing its whole economy down."[1]

The contention that industrialization and urbanization are incompatible with rigid socioeconomic and political inequality has been disproved over several centuries and across several continents, but the American South presents a textbook example of how the forces of what we might call economic modernization may not only adapt to antidemocratic social and political institutions, such as segregation and disfranchisement, but actually help to perpetuate them. As we shall see, in the southern context of the late nineteenth century, the appropriate question seemed to be not whether segregation could survive industrialization but whether industrialization could even proceed without segregation. Six years after the *Brown v. Board of Education* decision, however, Nicholls explained that the white South's still-resolute refusal to abandon segregation was typical of a "primitive rural folk society" where "laws . . . follow customs." Here Nicholls reflected a prevailing historical and sociological vision in which the struggle against Jim Crow pitted the progressive statutes and institutions, or "stateways," of a modern, urban-industrial society against the deeply rooted "folkways" of a backward, rural, and agricultural one.[2]

If old Mr. Webster is to be believed, "folkways" are "the ways of living and acting in a human group, built up without conscious design but serving as compelling guides of conduct." Defined in this fashion, the term implies a broad and largely internalized consensus among the "folk" of a society on the appropriateness or necessity of certain forms of behavior that have been legitimized by a common group experience. The language employed here is actually attributed to turn-of-the-century sociologist William Graham Sumner, whose insistence that laws were no match for "ancient custom" had evolved into a widely held popular and scholarly belief that "stateways cannot change folkways." Expressed in what Sumner's fellow sociologist Henry Franklin Giddings called a transcendent "consciousness of kind," this belief in the immutability of folkways was reflected in the words of Justice Henry Billings Brown, whose 1896 *Plessy v. Ferguson* opinion upholding separate facilities for blacks and whites had noted that "legislation is powerless to eradicate racial instincts, or to abolish distinctions based on physical differences."[3]

Nearly sixty years later, hailing the *Brown* decision's invalidation of *Plessy* as good news for "all God's chillun," a *New York Times* editorial nonetheless cautioned that "[t]he folkways in Southern communities will have to be adapted to new conditions if white and negro children, together with white and negro teachers, are to enjoy not only equal facilities but the same facilities in the same schools." Although he did not share the *Times*'s enthusiasm for the Court's ruling, the editor of the *Cavalier Daily* at the University of Virginia agreed that the decision was in conflict with long-standing southern custom: "To many people the decision is contrary to a way of life and violates the way they have thought since 1619."[4]

Just a few months later students, faculty, and members of the Charlottesville community would hear a decidedly different message from C. Vann Woodward, a Johns Hopkins University historian who had prepared a research brief for the NAACP legal team that had argued the *Brown* case. In the James Richards Lectures delivered at the University of Virginia in the fall of 1954 and rushed into print the following spring as *The Strange Career of Jim Crow*, Woodward observed that "the national discussion over the questions of how deeply rooted, how ineradicable, and how unamenable to change the segregation practices really are is being conducted against a background of faulty or inadequate historical information. And some of the most widely held sociological theories regarding segregation are based on erroneous history." Many years later Woodward explained that at the time the Court declared de jure segregation unconstitutional, the majority of whites, not just in the South but throughout the nation, seemed "assured that this was the way things had always been, that it was because of Southern folkways, that colored people themselves preferred it that way, and anyway there was nothing that could be done to change it."[5]

Attributing a society's resistance to change to the strength of prevailing folkways assumes that social and cultural continuity are simply the natural state of things rather than a reflection of particular individual or class interests or preferences. However, as Barrington Moore Jr. put it, in order "[t]o maintain and transmit a value system" over time, "human beings . . . [have been] punched, bullied, sent to jail, thrown into concentration camps, cajoled, bribed, made into heroes, encouraged to read newspapers, stood up against a wall and shot, and sometimes even taught sociology." Therefore, Webster's notion that folkways "are built up without conscious design" ignores what Moore calls "the concrete interests and privileges that are served by . . . the entire complicated process of transmitting culture from one generation to the next" while accepting at face value the very "justifications that ruling groups generally offer for their most brutal conduct."[6]

The surest sign that a particular social practice has become hard to justify is an effort by its defenders to stress its ancient origins, regardless of how old it may actually be. In the case of segregation the effectiveness of this defense may be discerned in the remarks of Democratic presidential candidate Adlai Stevenson, who, two years after the initial *Brown* decision and with images of the brutal murder of Emmett Till still vivid, warned a black audience that "we must proceed gradually, not upsetting habits or traditions that are older than the Republic."[7]

Intent on undermining those who tried to invest racial separation with the implied legitimacy of a folkway whose strength and immunity to stateways were both derived from and reflected in its antiquity, Woodward painted a different picture of the origins of segregation, one in which rigid constraints on racial interaction had not emerged in tandem with slavery because the former would have been both unnecessary and impractical in the presence of the latter. He conceded that segregation of schools, churches, and the military had become commonplace during Reconstruction, but contended that instead of immediately restoring a rigid, white-dominated racial hierarchy, the collapse of the Republican regimes had led to an era of general inconsistency and fluidity in black-white relations.[8]

Woodward drew on a smattering of travelers' accounts and newspaper reports of blacks and whites intermingling without incident on trains or in public spaces to argue that "through the seventies and eighties and up into the nineties the Negro enjoyed a degree of freedom from segregation that he was not to enjoy in the twentieth-century South." This period of relative fluidity was cut short, however, by the various Jim Crow laws that began to appear in the region during the 1890s. Hence, from Woodward's perspective, in this case stateways had, at the very least, changed folkways significantly and, arguably, even created them by forging random impulses to discriminate into a cohesive and uniform regionwide pattern.[9]

Woodward's contention, then, as John W. Cell summarized it, was that "[s]egregation, a comparatively new system of race relations that had been characteristic neither of slavery, nor of Reconstruction, nor even of the era of Redemption after the 1870s, had been imposed rather suddenly by law. In the powerful mythology of Southern history, however, it had become tradition." Not only was segregation an "invented tradition," but it was a relatively recent one at that, so much so that as Woodward looked about in the mid-1950s, he realized that "many of those who are currently defending the Jim Crow laws as ancient and immemorial folkways are older than the laws they are defending."[10]

In arguing that after Reconstruction "the Negro" had been "effectively restored to an inferior position through laws and practices, now dignified as 'custom and tradition,'" the NAACP lawyers in the *Brown* case had drawn heavily on Woodward's interpretation three years earlier in *Origins of the New South*. At that time Woodward had suggested that "coercion of sovereign white opinion" had been a "more pervasive" force in creating segregation than had "state and local law." In *The Strange Career of Jim Crow*, however, he took great pains to present segregation as more a product of codification than custom, stressing the gravity of bestowing the "majesty of law" on whites' previously erratic and ill-defined inclination to separate themselves from blacks. By arguing that things had once (and not so long ago) been different, Woodward was clearly implying that it was reasonable to believe that they could be so again: if the application of law had altered patterns of racial interaction for the worse, could the same means not be used to alter these patterns again for the better?[11]

As Richard H. King noted, Woodward was clearly attempting to "demythologize the existing social and legal institutions that regulated race relations" as a means of encouraging Americans, white or black, southern or otherwise, to believe that enough pressure applied at the right points might topple these institutions. Woodward also suggested that segregation was not an inevitable outcome. There had been "forgotten alternatives"; if the at least tentatively biracial Populist challenge had succeeded, or if conservative white paternalists had not capitulated to a rising post-Populist tide of virulent white racism, things might have gone otherwise.[12]

Woodward had pointed out in *Origins of the New South* that "the barriers of racial discrimination mounted in direct ratio with the tide of political democracy among whites." As he saw it, after the Populists were thwarted by the manipulation of black votes and the bugaboo of black domination, many lower-class whites had simply redirected the fury of their frustrations and insecurities against the most convenient scapegoat, demanding the complete social, political, and economic resubjugation of African Americans. Many blacks and northern liberals embraced Woodward's "redneck-centric" interpretation of the origins of the Jim Crow system, primarily because it gave them hope. Surely, the better-bred, better-fed, and better-read class of whites, whom George W. Cable had described in 1885 as the "Silent South," would reassert itself eventually, especially if these whites were prodded by the courts and pressured by national public opinion and a federal government increasingly sensitive to the contradiction of talking democracy abroad while tolerating apartheid at home. Beyond that, the South's ongoing economic and educational progress would both enlarge the potentially dominant white "better element" and force it to see the Jim Crow system for the crippling and embarrassing anachronism that it was.[13]

Woodward would later protest that many in the huge general readership that his book attracted had ignored his scholarly cautions and qualifications and leapt to the conclusion that, owing to Jim Crow's still relatively tender roots in law rather than long-standing custom, he should be a relatively easy mark. In reality, however, Woodward's academic peers seemed to read him much the same way. In reviewing *Strange Career,* African American historian Rayford W. Logan thought that the new cracks in Jim Crow's armor might be attributable to "the relative recency of many of the segregation laws" and reasoned that "additional breakdowns of the barriers may be easier for the same reason." Meanwhile, black sociologist E. Franklin Frazier praised Woodward for demonstrating that "the race problem was *made* and that men can *unmake* it, as they are attempting it today." That both Logan and Frazier, who clearly knew that Jim Crow was one tough customer, could come away from Woodward's book spouting such optimism surely raises questions about how its author could possibly have believed that his eloquent and skillful attack on the historical and cultural legitimacy of segregation could have been interpreted otherwise. Certainly, if it had been read as the careful and restrained piece of scholarship that Woodward later insisted he had intended to write, there is reason to doubt whether *The Strange Career of Jim Crow* would have gone on to sell more than a million copies. Nor would it have been likely to become such an inspiration to those committed to unmaking the race problem that the Reverend Martin Luther King Jr. reportedly called it "the historical Bible of the civil rights movement."[14]

Woodward explained that he had challenged contemporary opinion about the origins of the Jim Crow system because it rested "on shaky historical foundations," but his own attempt to rectify this situation was hardly anchored in a mother lode of documentation itself. In fact, as David Potter pointed out, Woodward's sweeping contention that "an era of experiment and variety in race relations" had preceded the emergence of the Jim Crow laws at the end of the nineteenth century rested on a grand total of three travelers' accounts (two northern, one British), two editorials, and two observations by southerners, one white and one black. From this exceedingly slim sample, I might add, Woodward had selectively drawn only material favorable to his point of view, to the exclusion of other contradictory evidence, sometimes within the same or adjoining paragraph within the same source.[15]

Beyond Woodward's use of his scant evidence was his willingness to rely so heavily on anecdotal reports from travelers who were not familiar with any possible pattern of day-to-day habits and attitudes toward race relations within a specific local context. The outwardly calm and even amicable conditions that a traveler observed on a single day or even a single journey might well have been contradicted by scenes of violence and vituperation witnessed in the same setting by another traveler on a different day or a different sojourn. Without more evidence and a more systematic examination of it, it was impossible to know whether what Woodward saw as a pattern of "inconsistency" would be better described as simply a collection of aberrations.

What Potter called "the urgency of Woodward's desire to find answers in the past which would aid in the quest for solutions of the problems of the present" is readily apparent in *The Strange Career of Jim Crow*. In fact, Potter observed, at certain points, Woodward's personal commitment to "liberal goals" appeared to get the better of his normally keen sense of "historical realism." A case in point is his determination to set his analysis of the origins of Jim Crow within the context of contemporary popular debate about whether stateways could influence folkways. This led him not only to exaggerate the long-term importance of distinguishing between the two but to place more emphasis on "when" and "how" segregation arose than "why." In the latter case he inadvertently provoked a full generation of scholarly inquiry and argument largely circumscribed by an approach that he had taken in order to reach a nonscholarly audience.[16]

One of the earliest and most effective critics of this central thrust of Woodward's argument was Joel Williamson, whose study of blacks in South Carolina during Reconstruction led him to conclude in 1965 that racial separation had been enforced by habit and custom long before it had been written into law. "Well before the end of Reconstruction," Williamson wrote, segregation had already "crystallized into a comprehensive pattern which, in its essence, remained unaltered until the middle of the twentieth century." Williamson did not address the stateways-versus-folkways debate in so many words, but he did observe that by the time South Carolina was readmitted to the Union in 1868, the South had "little need to establish legally a separation which already existed in fact," especially when doing so would have violated federal civil rights legislation then on the books and might have given "needless offense to influential elements in the North." In any event, the central issue for Williamson was not the actual "physical separation of the races" itself but the sense that "the real color line lived in the minds of individuals of each race, and it had achieved full growth even before freedom for the Negro was born."[17]

Where Woodward had sounded a note of optimism about the possibility for change in the immediate aftermath of *Brown*, Williamson's decidedly more sobering vision of an older and more deeply rooted white racial antipathy helped to explain why, a bloody, strife-ridden decade after the decision, roughly 98 percent of the South's black children were still attending all-black schools. Like Woodward, Williamson also drew heavily on anecdotal sources, but if one is to rely on such documentation, having a lot of it is obviously better than having a little, and Williamson and others who challenged Woodward's interpretation ultimately won the sheer weight-of-evidence contest hands down. By 1982 John Cell could legitimately conclude that Woodward's "suggestion that the South before the 1890s was in practice a comparatively open society, in which white and black competed on surprisingly equal terms, contradicts most, though certainly not all, of the available evidence about the lives of most Southerners in the generation after the Civil War." In 2004 Michael J. Klarman's survey of the secondary literature on the origins of Jim Crow barely nodded to Woodward's interpretation in a footnote while proclaiming rather definitively in the text that "what formal segregation replaced for the most part was not integration, but informal segregation," and thus "Jim Crow law reflected, more than it produced, segregationist practices."[18]

Hoping to intensify the contemporary assault on the Jim Crow system, Woodward and other civil-rights-era historians presented segregation as the worst possible racial outcome for the freedmen. Moreover, it was also hard in the 1950s and 1960s to gaze upon the demagoguery of an Orval Faubus or a Ross Barnett and believe that segregation could have been motivated by anything other than the incorrigible racism, ignorance, and hostility to progress that both epitomized and explained the white South's backwardness. This absolutist historical perspective was perfectly understandable at a time when people were marching in the streets and dying in the shadows in order to right an enormous wrong. Even today it is sometimes difficult to see issues of black and white in anything other than black and white, but such an approach ultimately obstructs our view of the complexity and unevenness of the historical processes of racial discrimination in the South and throughout the nation, for that matter.

By the end of the 1970s Howard Rabinowitz seemed a bit more detached from the passions of the civil rights era when he argued that "[t]he issue is not just when segregation appeared but what it replaced." That, in his view, was the outright exclusion of blacks from public institutions, organizations, and accommodations that had begun in the antebellum era and resurfaced in southern cities in the interlude between the end of the war and the onset of congressional Reconstruction in 1867. Blacks had protested this exclusion, and insofar as possible they had also responded to it by forming organizations and institutions of their own. Still, one need not accept the premise behind segregation to understand that a South with racially separate public spaces and facilities was preferable to one where neither was even available to blacks.[19]

The possibility that legally mandated racial separation might be something other than the worst possible manifestation of southern white racism was reinforced a few years later, when John Cell offered a bold new synthesis that challenged the traditional view of segregation as "the stubborn persistence into the capitalist era of the 'irrational' legacy of the past." In Cell's view, as the "highest stage of white supremacy," segregation had arisen not as a simple expression of, but as a milder, more modern, and complex alternative to, the white racial extremism that had seemed to crest in the South at the end of the nineteenth century. Nor was it the handiwork of the self-styled political champions of the ignorant rural white masses. On the contrary, many of the earliest proponents of segregation had actually been northerners and Republicans. In South Carolina white Republicans like James L. Orr and B. O. Duncan had opposed integrated schools for fear that even the slightest racial friction might trigger an outburst of violence by white parents.[20]

Charged with disbursing the Peabody Fund's contributions to southern education, Barnas G. Sears saw "the curse of trying to have mixed schools" as a serious impediment to his work and was instrumental in having provisions for integrated education deleted from the Civil Rights Act of 1875 for fear that they would trigger a mass withdrawal of whites from the schools. It was not conspiratorial southern racists but northern philanthropists who had most often insisted on establishing separate colleges and industrial schools for blacks after Reconstruction. In doing so, they had sometimes faced stiff resistance, not from a tiny group of southern liberals but from vindictive racists like James K. Vardaman of Mississippi or South Carolina's Ben Tillman, who saw any form of education for blacks as not just a waste of time and money but downright dangerous.[21]

In general, the proponents of legally mandated segregation were not the likes of Vardaman and Tillman but other, more moderate, albeit racially paternalistic, men like Episcopal clergyman Edgar Gardner Murphy, who saw in the brutal and incendiary racial onslaughts of such demagogues "the contention that no negro shall learn, that no negro shall labor, and (by implication) that no negro shall live." The best way to save African Americans from these assailants and give them a chance to improve themselves, Murphy believed, was not to consign "the negro forever to a lower place but to accord him another place." Segregation, then, was simply an extension of the traditional wisdom that "good fences make good neighbors." Meanwhile, taking a more forthrightly pragmatic view, Henry W. Grady and other proponents of "New South" economic progress had endorsed segregation as the most effective means of achieving the racial stability requisite to establishing a modern industrial economy in the post-Reconstruction South.[22]

This position would have seemed unthinkable to white liberals of the civil rights era who believed that segregation was wholly incompatible with the notion of any sort of progress, social or economic. Yet, as Cell saw it, "segregation was closely associated with what we commonly regard as indexes of modernization." In practical terms, this meant urbanization, industrialization, and especially the dramatic emergence of an expanded and consolidated rail network.

The railroad served as both the literal and figurative vehicle of modernity. Rail travel wrested control of the schedule, speed, and circumstances of one's journey from the individual southerner and transferred it to an alien and detached corporation. Beyond that, the actual physical and social circumstances in which one traveled were now largely in the hands of the train's conductor, who was bound by no local allegiance or obligation and answerable only to his employer. As a systematic approach to reducing the racial uncertainties of this strange new environment, Jim Crow not only arrived in the South by train but was riding in first class. Most whites who traveled by rail sat in first class. By virtue of their economic circumstances, most blacks traveled second class, but those who could afford it sometimes opted for the first-class car, making it a setting where whites had little control over their contact with and proximity to blacks. Thus the rapid rise in rail travel trapped railroad executives between white passengers who objected vociferously and sometimes violently to sharing the limited confines of the first-class coach with blacks and black passengers whose numerous protests and lawsuits reflected their refusal to accept anything less than first-class accommodations after purchasing a first-class ticket. As historian Edward L. Ayers wrote, "Tough decisions forced themselves on the state legislatures of the South after the railroads came," resulting in "the first wave of segregation laws that affected virtually the entire South in anything like a uniform way." Nine southern states enacted railroad segregation laws between 1887 and 1891, and by 1896, when the *Plessy* verdict came down, only the Carolinas and Virginia lacked such provisions.[23]

Although some railroad spokesmen claimed to welcome an authoritative clarification of how they were to manage racial proximity on their trains, a number of railroad executives also resisted passage of separate coach laws on the grounds of cost and efficiency, and some even encouraged black passengers to challenge the constitutionality of these laws in court. The larger rail lines felt the cost of Jim Crow primarily in the mandatory allocation of separate cars or seating space. This gave the companies a built-in incentive to underestimate the African American percentage of their ridership, but the railroads generally contended that blacks accounted for less than 20 percent of local passengers and a significantly smaller fraction of interstate travelers. Thus mandatory separation helped to reduce the size of the black passenger population even further, and it also increased the incentives for skimping on the amount and quality of the space allocated to those blacks who did ride the trains. Laws requiring separate cars for each race obliged the railroads to calculate by color the usual percentage of passenger traffic on a particular stretch. An unexpected shift in these proportions as a result of special events such as fairs or court week could throw things out of kilter, however, requiring the company either to add a car or to move the passengers of one car en masse to another car, for example. In some cases the rail companies sought to achieve the requisite racial separation by using partitions or screens, but this practice led repeatedly to complaints by whites that such an arrangement failed to provide adequate distance from black travelers. Meanwhile, black passengers objected to being separated by nothing but a flimsy partition from the noisy, unruly whites who were using the remainder of the car as a smoking car. For all the operational headaches that Jim Crow legislation imposed, however, the bottom line for railroad management was the comfort and satisfaction of the white travelers who made up the overwhelming majority of their clientele, and railroad executives gradually accepted the expense of guaranteeing racial separation on their trains as a cost of doing business in the South.[24]

It is worth noting that the situation was a bit different on streetcars and local suburban rail lines where African Americans made up a larger percentage of the riders. Because black boycotts or the simple loss of black patronage could and did pinch many local companies severely, they often dragged their feet in implementing and enforcing the new legislation mandating racial separation on public conveyances. Although Woodward suggested that incidences of racial intermingling were largely a thing of the past in the public arena as soon as the segregation statutes were imposed, passengers on streetcars or short-line railroads in a number of southern cities might well have described numerous scenes of black-white proximity long after the Jim Crow laws were officially on the books. The Georgia law requiring racial separation on all streetcars and interurban railroads went into effect in 1891, but seven years later the Augusta Railway and Electric Company had made no move to enforce it, and the company's president even claimed that he knew of "no such law on the statute books." Meanwhile in Atlanta a full fifteen years after the law had been passed and a decade after the *Plessy v. Ferguson* decree, at least one local railway company was still dragging its feet on enforcing segregation on its lines. Citing additional examples from states like Florida and Tennessee, Jennifer Robock has concluded that, initially at least, a great many southern streetcar companies simply ignored their state's Jim Crow law or "blatantly refused to enforce it."[25]

Be it streetcar or interstate rail line, the close quarters imposed by public transportation provided a microcosmic foreshadowing of the potentially explosive tensions from interracial contact that modern urban life and industrial work would surely bring. Hence, as Cell pointed out, despite Jim Crow's traditional image as an embodiment of the rabid racism of rural whites, he was not "born and bred among 'rednecks' in the country. First and foremost he was a city slicker." Rigid residential segregation had long been a fact of life in the urban North. Because the New South's fast-growing new cities would lead the way in bringing the races in contact with each other in unfamiliar surroundings and circumstances, these dynamic locales seemed most in need of the structure and order promised by systematic racial separation. Not surprisingly, then, segregation made its earliest and most visible impact not in older, more racially "settled" cities such as Charleston or New Orleans but in upstart boomtowns like Atlanta and Birmingham. By 1910, for example, indexes of racially dissimilar residential patterns showed that Birmingham was approximately five times more segregated than Charleston. Far from a capitulation to the past, in the New South of the late nineteenth and early twentieth centuries, segregation was the harbinger of a vibrant and dynamic future.[26]

African Americans' insistence on getting the accommodations that they paid for played a key role in forcing legislators to mandate segregation on the region's railways. Efforts by blacks throughout the 1880s to expand their rights and opportunities across a broad social, political, and economic spectrum helped to convince southern whites that they could reestablish a stable, comprehensive racial order only by making white supremacy a matter not simply of custom but of law. Joel Williamson noted in 1965 that the contours of racial interaction always shifted when what he called "vigorous assaults by one side or the other forced the enemy to yield his forward trenches and to alter slightly the precise line of the color front." More recently, Steven Hahn's sweeping study of black political activity in the postbellum South led him to conclude that the Jim Crow system was actually not so much "an imposition . . . as a product of struggle."[27]

Urbanization and industrialization and greater black mobility and aggressiveness were making access to certain spaces increasingly competitive, and by allowing whites to order and control these contested spaces, segregation became both an instrument and symbol of white power and status in the New South. However, the racism that lay at the heart of Jim Crow legislation should not obscure the connection between moving to control—and effectively limit—racial interaction and the broader reliance on governmental authority to regulate or restrict human and corporate behavior that we typically associate with the modernizing reforms of the Progressive era.

Beyond their obvious racial ramifications, segregation statutes, which applied first to the railroads and then to other public conveyances and spaces, were more than anything else indicative of what Robert Wiebe called the Progressive era's "search for order." Relying on white coercion to sort out interracial contact might work in small towns and rural areas, but in the dynamic fast lane of southern progress, such a laissez-faire approach left too much to chance, too much ambiguity, too much opportunity for disruption and confrontation. Before passage of the Jim Crow statutes, first-class rail travel for blacks was generally, at the very least, "dangerous and uncertain," as Edward Ayers put it, because "[e]ach road had its own customs and policy, and the events on the train might depend on the proclivity of the conductor or, worse, the mood and makeup of the white passengers who happened to be on board." Ultimately, it seemed far better to be proactive than reactive. Barbara Young Welke explained that, like other more traditional progressive regulatory or supervisory measures that were grounded in a fundamentally negative view of human nature, "the segregation statutes took prejudice, hatred, and the likelihood of violence when the races mixed for granted and sought an administrative solution." Certainly, Ayers concluded, "[r]ail road segregation was not a throwback to old-fashioned racism; indeed, segregation became to whites a badge of sophisticated, modern, managed race relations."[28]

Much the same was true of disfranchisement, which as Howard Rabinowitz argued, actually proved to be the cornerstone of southern progressivism. By the end of the nineteenth century, some of the white South's ostensibly most advanced thinkers had embraced suffrage limitations as an absolute necessity, insisting that by eliminating white competition for black votes, they would reduce both the racial tension and electoral fraud that had turned postbellum southern politics into what one critic called a "perpetual knife fight and stomping contest." In short, disfranchisement was supposed to bring the same sort of order to southern politics that segregation was to impose on southern society. Some New South intellectuals even saw suffrage restriction as leading to the rise of two-party politics, because, freed from the divisive and potentially threatening presence of the black vote, southern whites could calmly and soberly entertain the Republican Party's platform and principles solely on their merits. The likely upshot of the emergence of two-party political competition, they reasoned, would be the South's full and speedy reintegration into the national political system.[29]

Suffice it to say, the ultimate effect of disfranchisement on southern and national politics proved to be a bit different from what its architects had promised. Sure enough, the disfranchisement statutes kept almost all blacks and many poor whites away from the polls. In so doing, however, these laws effectively concentrated power even more tightly in the grip of those who had the most to gain from perpetuating the Democratic Party's political hegemony. With the Democrats comfortably ensconced as Dixie's party of no other choice, electoral participation plummeted, but corruption still flourished as fierce intraparty factional struggles quickly became the order of the day. Contrary to expectations, issues and ideological differences fell by the wayside as one-party elections forced all aspirants into a single Democratic primary that often featured a huge field of candidates. Not surprisingly, victory often went to the one who managed to catch the electorate's attention by yelling "white supremacy" the loudest and generally acting the biggest fool.

By rewarding demagoguery, disfranchisement heightened rather than reduced racial tensions. In fact, the debates about suffrage restrictions themselves usually featured incendiary racist rhetoric that often exploded in firestorms of white-on-black violence, typified by the horrific Atlanta riot of 1906, some of whose black victims were piled, symbolically enough, at the foot of a statue of New South prophet Henry Grady. The Atlanta riot hardly gave evidence of the racial stability that the disfranchisers had promised, but stripping the vote from blacks and many poor whites did achieve one primary goal sought by Grady and his New South counterparts. The white South did reintegrate itself into national politics and on its own terms. Insulated from the masses of black and white voters, reactionary southern senators and members of Congress returned to Washington year after year. By using their seniority to thwart any and all initiatives that might undermine their powerful Black Belt and corporate patrons, these solidly entrenched southern Democrats managed to preserve not just white supremacy over blacks but the supremacy of the South's white economic elite over the masses of both races.

Not surprisingly, the strategy for maintaining this elite supremacy did not entail generous support for educating the aforesaid masses. Then as now, intellectuals insisted that educational progress was the key to economic progress, but, as Gavin Wright has explained, employers of a predominantly low-wage, unskilled southern workforce had little reason to believe that they could recover any significant investment in schooling their workers. In fact, employers feared that "too much" education would actually "demoralize" their employees by making them dissatisfied with their current status and condition. This concern was especially apparent among those who depended on black workers. Educational opportunities for African Americans who labored in the mines and steel mills around Birmingham had been notably better than those available elsewhere, and when World War I interrupted the flow of European immigration into the northern states, the black workers of the Birmingham area were among the first to head north in pursuit of greater opportunity and freedom.[30]

When liberal critics contended that the last thing the backward and impoverished South needed was the additional cost of two-school systems, they failed to consider the sizable savings accruing from severe budgetary discrimination against black schools. Creating a unitary school system meant equalizing spending and capital investment across racial lines. In order to accomplish this, unless already meager expenditures on white education were to be slashed in the process, a state like Georgia, which in 1930 was spending an average of approximately $45 on each white pupil and $8 on each black pupil, would have needed to boost its total educational outlays by about 40 percent.[31]

According to the classic economic model, racial discrimination should quickly succumb to the competitive pressures of the modern industrial marketplace because it prevents employers from getting labor at the lowest possible cost. In postbellum southern manufacturing, however, a worker's skin color typically had less direct influence on his wages per se than on the type of job that he held or the industry in which he worked. As Wright has shown, there was surprisingly little discrimination in the South's market for agricultural wage labor because landowners refused to pay white workers more than they would have to pay black ones. Meanwhile, the relatively easy flow of individual wage workers (primarily young unmarried males) from farm to factory and back again helped to insure that southern industrial wages followed a similar pattern. As what Wright called "the classic prototype of a labor surplus region," the postbellum South could offer plenty of unskilled workers for its nascent manufacturing sector at or near the relatively nondiscriminatory agricultural wage, thereby giving industrial employers an ample supply of white workers at what was effectively a black worker's pay.[32]

In a region where white racial animosities and anxieties were so volatile, the political sustainability of such a surprisingly color-blind industrial wage system was dependent on substituting physical distance for economic distance. Hence segregation operated by industry as well as by job. For example, the workforce in textiles and furniture was overwhelmingly white, while tobacco and timber workers were overwhelmingly black. Because of the general availability of whites at the same wage, the initial exclusion of blacks from the textile industry cost employers little or nothing at the outset, and when, over time, the requirements of textile work became specialized enough to command somewhat higher compensation, these additional wage costs were deemed insufficient to justify starting from scratch to train black workers who had never before seen the inside of a cotton mill.

Meanwhile, within an industry that employed workers of both races, spatial separation was the order of the day, and the more mechanized the production process became, the easier it was to segment. The problem for black workers in these industries was that, although they received roughly the same pay as whites in unskilled jobs, other better-paying and more promising positions were simply not available to blacks. Although this practice was racist and wrongheaded, its immediate economic costs to employers were minimal so long as there were sufficient numbers of white workers competent to fill the higher-echelon jobs that had become their racial birthright. Had the region's economy grown rapidly enough to fuel demand for more workers than could be secured efficiently without setting color barriers aside, racial separation and discrimination might have imposed significant costs on the process. As Cell observed, however, "the South's pattern of industrialization adapted so naturally to Jim Crow that the two phenomena soon became apparently inseparable."[33]

The same could be said of the effort to convince northern investors to provide the capital necessary to expand and accelerate southern industrial development. It was no mere coincidence that, as the last vestiges of northern support for Reconstruction collapsed in 1877, the *Philadelphia Telegraph* pointed to a South where "land, labor, fuel, water power, and building facilities are cheap" and "the way to clear and large profits is open." Eager New South boosters seldom missed a chance to invite their better-heeled northern brethren to come on down and exploit their region's surplus labor and abundant raw materials, but a potential impediment to the marriage of northern money and know-how and southern labor and natural resources was the instability of race relations in the region. Accordingly, as Paul Gaston has shown, segregation became a vital element of Henry Grady's "New South Creed." More than a decade before the *Plessy* verdict, Grady had insisted in a widely read *Century Magazine* article that the U.S. Constitution mandated "equal accommodations for the two races, but separate." This provision should apply "in every theater," and, Grady believed, "the same rule should be observed in railroads, schools and elsewhere."[34]

As Grady and his New South cohort sought northern industrial capital, they argued that racial and political home rule for southern whites—in effect, the rolling back of the tragically misguided policies of Reconstruction—was the prerequisite for improving the South's investment climate and facilitating the region's rapid reintegration into the national economy. Segregation was vital to the success of the New South movement, because a stable racial climate was essential to a stable "labor climate," which, in the euphemistic rhetoric of New South boosters, actually meant an abundance of cheap, dependable, and docile workers. As the legacy of Reconstruction began to unravel and the federal courts pitched in to validate the process, by restricting southern racial interaction, segregation promised to ease tensions not just between southern blacks and southern whites but between southern whites and northern whites as well, thus facilitating the flow of capital from North to South.

Likewise, by helping to forge a relatively static, conservative southern political order, disfranchisement allowed New South propagandists to assure northern investors that their enjoyment of minimal taxation and untrammeled access to cheap labor and natural resources would not be in jeopardy every time an election rolled around. Certainly, the commercial and industrial leaders of the New South had little reason to object to the political neutralization of the black and lower-class white voters who had been drawn to the Populist cause. After all, they might well be tempted to embrace other crusades for economic democratization and expanded social services that could undermine the attractions of minimal wages, minimal taxation, and minimal regulation in a region desperate to secure external investment capital. The less voting by such people, the better, because, as Henry Grady had warned, this kind of activist politics was anathema to "investors" and could only lead to "such oppressive laws . . . that capital is kept away."[35]

Attracting capital and reassuring capitalists was a primary objective of the 1895 Cotton States Exposition in Atlanta. A year before the Supreme Court validated segregation, the event marked the first public endorsement of the emerging New South's racial order by a southern black leader. Booker T. Washington assured a segregated exposition audience brimming with influential whites that "in all things that are purely social we can be as separate as fingers, yet one as the hand in all things essential to actual progress." In this sense the exposition represented a sort of coming-out party for what Grace Hale has called the New South's "fusion of racial order and economic progress."[36]

While some New South communities distributed promotional material that simply excluded blacks altogether or showed them, with little or no comment, in the roles of domestic servants or agricultural workers, other communities actually tried to turn segregation into a selling point. An ad touting Richmond, Virginia, in 1912 boasted of "separate schools for whites and blacks, separate churches, hotels, railroad coaches, and in fact, no intermingling of the races socially, though relations otherwise are amicable and friendly." Thus, Hale concludes, the "culture of segregation" offered a means for the South to be assimilated into the economic mainstream of "modern America" by providing "a way to embrace modernism and also contain it, a way to allow greater fluidity for other identities even while attempting to hold race fast."[37]

Edward Ayers summed up the complex and dynamic context in which segregation emerged quite nicely when he noted that it was "the product of no particular class, of no wave of hysteria or displaced frustration, no rising tide of abstract racism, no new ideas about race. Like everything else in the New South, segregation grew out of concrete situations, out of technological, demographic, economic, and political changes that had unforeseen and often unintended social consequences." If we are to understand the Jim Crow system as it stood, still intact and formidable, in 1954, then we must look beyond the tenacity of the racial folkways of rural white southerners in the face of the social and political encroachments of urbanization and industrialization. Indeed, we should examine the role of racial discrimination, not as an impediment but as an integral facilitating factor that was deeply embedded within the actual process of economic modernization as it unfolded in the South during the last quarter of the nineteenth century and the first half of the twentieth. Ironically, despite its contributions to southern reintegration into the national economy, this institutionalized system of apartheid also played a key role in sustaining the South's identity as a region apart from the rest of American society.[38]

The origins of a pattern of behavior are sometimes discernible in the factors that bring it to an end. Sharecropping, for example, began disappearing in the 1930s when government incentives to reduce crop acreage gave previously cash-strapped landlords the capital they needed to move toward a more cost-effective reliance on day labor. Likewise, by the late 1950s, segregation, which had been held out as the best assurance of racial stability for the post-Reconstruction South, had become a breeding ground for the tension and conflict it had supposedly been implemented to prevent. Now a catalyst for disruptive protests and retaliatory violence, it threatened to undermine southern political and civic leaders' efforts to build on the economic momentum generated by World War II by adding better-paying firms to the region's low-wage industrial base. It was surely no coincidence that relatively peaceful desegregation proved more likely in cities like Atlanta and Charlotte where local elites were strongly committed to economic growth than in places like New Orleans and Birmingham where they were not.

Although Jim Crow would cling to life a while longer in the economically languid countryside, he effectively met his demise where he had been conceived—at the cutting edge of southern economic development. However, the end of his strange career was not an inevitable side-effect of the South's crusade for economic growth. If racial segregation arose in no small measure as a response to the aggressiveness of the first postbellum generation of African Americans in exercising their new freedoms, its collapse was no less attributable to the actions of another generation of activists who held the desire for a more developed southern economy hostage to their demands for a more developed southern society in which racial injustice would have no place.

2 Down on *Brown*

*Revisionist Critics and the History
That Might Have Been*

As I surveyed the predictable flood of media assessments
of the fifty-year legacy of the *Brown v. Board of Education* decision, I
was struck by what seemed to be the overwhelmingly negative tone
of these appraisals. In this case, as in so many others, historical and
contemporary opinions show remarkable convergence. *Brown* has
never been without its critics, of course, particularly on the right,
but in 1994 University of Virginia law professor Michael Klarman
emerged as the point man in a naysaying liberal revisionist assault
on the perception that the *Brown* decision enabled and energized
the civil rights movement. In fact, Klarman has argued that instead
of furthering the cause of racial equality, the ruling may actually
have set it back, at least temporarily. By provoking a virulent white
"backlash," Klarman suggests, the *Brown* decree actually aborted an
ongoing "indigenous Southern racial transformation" sparked by
the accelerating urbanization and industrialization and intensify-
ing demands of African Americans for racial justice that had
marked the first decade after World War II.[1]

Klarman has not been content simply with charging that *Brown*
effectively reversed "what had been steady black progress in the
region." He has also argued that its primary contribution to the
cause of civil rights actually came not in inspiring the protests of
the ensuing decade but in angering the southern whites whose ugly
and violent response to these protests eventually generated massive
national public pressure for federal action against racial discrimination. In one way or another, Klarman's arguments have been

anticipated, adopted, or affirmed by several other scholarly critics of the *Brown* decision, including prominent legal scholars Gerald Rosenberg, Mark Tushnet, Charles Ogletree, and Derrick Bell, who contends that the *Brown* ruling actually produced "advances greater for whites than for blacks." I have heard these arguments many times, and my studied, scholarly response to them remains, "Say what?"[2]

Surely, no one who has studied the history of the South in the twentieth century could argue that the region remained unchanged in the generation before the *Brown* decision. World War II was a culminating event in what had been a roughly thirty-year "turning period" in southern life, punctuated by numerous shocks, stresses, and strains, including the invasion of the boll weevil, the outmigration of an estimated 1.5 million southern blacks between 1915 and 1940, the economic upheaval of the Great Depression, and the ensuing agricultural and demographic restructuring of the New Deal.

During World War II the hypocrisy of sending U.S. troops to prevent all of Europe from falling under the control of a racist dictator while tolerating a racially repressive and thoroughly undemocratic regional subculture at home had simply proved too blatant to ignore. "To a nation fighting totalitarianism abroad," Morton Sosna observed, "Jim Crow became an embarrassment." Meanwhile, not only had NAACP membership increased ninefold during the war, but black veterans had returned home demanding a total and immediate end to Jim Crow.[3]

Still, Klarman's contention that "World War II's contribution to progressive racial change cannot be overstated" is, in fact, an overstatement itself, especially when the short-term white reaction to the war's potentially disruptive influence is considered. Former Mississippi congressman Frank Smith observed that "[m]ore young men came home from World War II with a sense of purpose than from any other American venture," but it did not necessarily follow that they all returned with the same sense of purpose. For every

Medgar Evers who came back hell-bent for justice, there was a Byron De La Beckwith, the former marine who killed him, or a Robert "Tut" Patterson, the one-time paratrooper who founded the segregationist Citizen's Council. As it had after World War I, racial violence, along with the resurgence of the Ku Klux Klan and the appearance of various other hate groups, reflected white fears that returning black servicemen might actually try to exercise some of the rights they had just risked their lives to defend.[4]

It was certainly true that returning white veterans demanding better government and more and better jobs played a key role in a number of "G.I. revolts" that ousted long-ensconced political rings in state and local governments across the South. The emergent good-government sorts definitely cringed at the racist rabble-rousing of the Gene Talmadges and Theodore G. Bilbos, but from Augusta to New Orleans to Little Rock the cry for reform stopped well short of even a hint that Jim Crow must go. At best, none of this new breed of better-element, business-oriented, post–World War II southern politicians ever got past ineffective calls for adherence to the "equal" component of the "separate but equal" principle that had seldom commanded more than lip service from whites since its enunciation by the Supreme Court in 1896.

Those who argue that the South was on the brink of an indigenous racial transformation before the *Brown* decision hold that the New Deal–inspired and World War II–accelerated mechanization of southern agriculture and the resultant slackening of demand for farm labor translated directly into less repressive conditions for blacks, because, as Klarman puts it, "Jim Crow imperatives became less exigent." This assumption is based on such historical oversimplifications as Derrick Bell's breezy reference to "the original agricultural basis for the Jim Crow social system."[5]

There is no denying that the southern racial system functioned as a means of labor control, but it was about a great deal more than hemming in field hands. The beginning of the Great Migration of blacks out of the South during the second decade of the twentieth century had seemed to spur labor-conscious white employers to use their influence to end the reign of racial terror that had dominated the two previous decades. However, as the need for black labor diminished in the late 1940s and 1950s, other developments actually gave whites *less* rather than more incentive to relax their chokehold on black freedom and opportunity. Some whites even responded to the Supreme Court's ruling in 1944 (*Smith v. Allwright*) that black voters could no longer be excluded from previously all-white Democratic primaries in the South by redoubling efforts to develop an effective mechanical cotton picker that would render their now electorally empowered black workers economically expendable and force them to leave the region before they could challenge white political supremacy. As one planter explained, "Mechanized farming will require only a fraction of the amount of labor which is required by the sharecropper system thereby tending to equalize the white and Negro population which would automatically make our racial problem easier to handle."[6]

The supercharged Southwide drive for industrial development that emerged after World War II was supposed to yield new and expanded opportunities for all southerners, but continued emphasis in promotional materials on a large pool of "Anglo-Saxon" labor signaled clearly enough that black employment was not exactly a priority for those who sought more industrial jobs and payrolls. In light of the recently enacted Voting Rights Act of 1965 and census numbers showing five thousand more blacks than whites in Yazoo County, Mississippi, local development officials candidly admitted that they were interested in creating new jobs only for whites.[7]

Arguing that a significant racial transformation was underway before the *Brown* decision, Gerald Rosenberg suggests that local business and political leaders had already recognized "the economic costs of segregation," and Klarman credits their efforts "to cultivate outside industrial investment" with "creating pressure for Southern compliance with national racial norms." This is absolutely correct but only if one is referring to the decade *after Brown,* when civil rights protests finally forced southern business and development leaders to choose between keeping segregation and losing much-needed new jobs and payrolls. The effort to sell the South to northern industrial investors had definitely picked up momentum before the *Brown* decree. In the absence of violence or disruptive protests, however, neither southern economic leaders nor the officials of incoming industries had given much indication that they considered segregation itself to be the least bit worrisome in terms of continued industrial growth.[8]

Incoming industries seemed to adapt nicely to prevailing patterns of segregation by industry and job, with only the most arduous, distasteful tasks open to blacks. The lumber industry continued to rely overwhelmingly on black workers, while textiles remained so lily-white that counties with heavy concentrations of cotton mills were typically those with correspondingly heavy rates of black out-migration. Because of the historic southern pattern of job discrimination, when the post–World War II South finally began to attract more skill-intensive, higher-wage industries, the initial impact on black workers was slight because they had been given so little opportunity to acquire the skills needed to move up the employment ladder. The same was truer still for supervisory positions. As of 1966 African Americans accounted for approximately 63 percent of the laborers in southern steel mills but less than 1 percent of the white-collar employees.[9]

Like the social scientists of the 1950s on whom they draw, those who argue that a southern racial revolution was underway before *Brown* not only put inordinate faith in industrialization and urbanization as "ineluctable forces" for social change, but they conjoin the two with little regard for the highly dispersed locational pattern of southern industries. With the advent of rural electrification, manufacturing executives had fanned out across the countryside seeking proximity to cheap, fresh-off-the-farm labor and distance from union organizers. As late as 1969, about 40 percent of the South's industrial plants were still in the rural and small-town settings where, most commentators seem to feel, whites were most resistant to racial change.[10]

Michael Klarman argues that before *Brown*, "[s]outhern whites had proved willing to make small concessions on racial issues that were less important to them than school segregation" and that, without *Brown*, "negotiation might have continued to produce gradual change without inciting white violence." Klarman even speculates that there might have been less hostility to a ruling that focused on black voting than to one that targeted "grade-school education," the area where white southerners were sure to be "most resistant." White southerners may have been less vehement in their opposition to black voting than to school integration, but their reactions to *Smith v. Allwright*'s invalidation of the white primary in 1944 suggest otherwise. These included purging registration lists and wholesale challenges of black voters, as well as new laws and constitutional amendments to keep blacks away from the polls. There were also not-so-veiled threats from Governor Eugene Talmadge that "wise Negroes will stay away from white folks' ballot boxes" in Georgia and inflammatory exhortations from Senator Theodore G. Bilbo that "every red-blooded Mississippian . . . use every means at their command" to keep blacks from voting. Not a single black resident cast a primary election ballot in Schley County, Georgia, in 1946 after the local state legislator effectively announced that any black voter would be a dead voter and stood outside the polls holding a shotgun to insure that his pronouncement was not taken lightly.[11]

Klarman notes that southern black voter registration "jumped by leaps and bounds in the 1940s," but the extent and effectiveness of white resistance to black voting may be reflected at least in part in the fact that while slightly more than one in six southern black adults were registered in 1948, fewer than one in ten actually managed to cast a ballot. In the presidential election of 1952 blacks accounted for only 6 percent of the total southern vote.[12]

Arguments that the *Brown* decision actually short-circuited a southern racial revolution also pay little attention to the Dixiecrat revolt of 1948, which demonstrated, six years before *Brown*, that a number of white southerners were already up in arms about the civil rights initiatives of the Truman administration. Less overtly race-conscious politicians like Jim Folsom in Alabama, Earl Long in Louisiana, and Sid McMath in Arkansas had managed to claim governorships in the wake of World War II, but anyone who sees the rise of a significant antisegregation sentiment among white politicians before the *Brown* decision has consulted a version of southern history that is unfamiliar to me.

At best, men like Folsom were playing defense rather than offense, calling for an end to violence and intimidation against black voters, preaching fairness in matters political and legal, trying to make the South's system of white supremacy more humane overall but doing little to suggest that they had either immediate or long-term intentions of overturning it. As Numan Bartley notes, in their neopopulistic efforts to focus on issues of "economics and class" rather than race, Long and Folsom "rejected much of the mythology and practice of white supremacy," but "neither governor espoused integration."[13]

Beyond that, the actual personal contact and communication between these white moderates and African American voters themselves was extremely limited. Typically, the moderates relied on black ministers and other intermediaries—in Folsom's case, his chauffeur—who worked to deliver the black vote as a single, unquestioning bloc. More moderate candidates had little incentive to provide black voters with the specifics of their views or agendas, because they knew full well that whatever they said sounded a lot better to their black constituents than the race-baiting of the other white candidates. As election time drew near, moderate white politicians studiously avoided any public identification with black voters; such meetings as were actually held were often convened by emissaries and, even then, usually only after it was good and dark.

When the *Brown* decision came down with all its accompanying uproar, Folsom's announcement that he would not force "the good colored people of Alabama to go to school with us white folks" was part joke but also part admission that he had no real strategy or enthusiasm for implementing the ruling in Alabama. Fittingly enough, when officials at the University of Alabama caved in to mob pressures to expel Autherine Lucy in 1956, Folsom was not around, having taken off with his cronies on an expedition to determine whether it was, in fact, truly possible to get too drunk to fish.[14]

There is little doubt that, as several critics of the Supreme Court decision have pointed out, the political outcry against moderates like Folsom grew much louder in the aftermath of *Brown*. However, if this anger stemmed from the perception that the federal government was finally prepared to take the problem of racial injustice seriously, then perhaps, before this unsettling revelation, southern racial moderates were simply not seen by their contemporaries as the significant threats to white supremacy that hindsighted critics of *Brown* now insist they were.[15]

Observing that "not since the Civil War had the need to remedy racial injustice been so firmly aligned with the country's vital interests at home and abroad," Derrick Bell is but one of the *Brown* decision's detractors who have suggested that competition with the Soviet Union for the allegiance of nonwhite peoples throughout the world would have assured Jim Crow's ultimate demise regardless of the Court's ruling in 1954. In the pre-*Brown* decade, however, anxiety about an international communist conspiracy cut two ways. As Mary L. Dudziak has pointed out, although concern about communist expansion abroad encouraged American leaders to address some of their country's racial wrongs, fear of communist subversion at home also wound up "silencing certain voices" by leaving "a very narrow space for criticism of the status quo."[16]

With the nation in the grip of what sometimes bordered on anti-communist hysteria, anyone who agitated against the racial status quo might be accused of taking orders directly from Moscow. The House Un-American Activities Committee mercilessly hounded members of the liberal Southern Conference for Human Welfare. When HUAC failed to find any real evidence of communism in the liberal group's ranks, the committee declared that the group was "perhaps the most deviously camouflaged Communist-front organization" in the United States. More telling still were the words of the moderate journalist Ralph McGill, who also accused the Southern Conference for Human Welfare of being "badly tainted at the top with Communism and fellow traveling." What some have called "the Cold War imperative" for racial change manifested itself overwhelmingly in meaningful but strictly circumscribed initiatives crafted not by liberal activists in Dixie but by seriously constrained policy wonks in Washington. Even these failed to gain the support of such ostensibly liberal southern political leaders as Claude Pepper and Frank Porter Graham, both of whom proved vulnerable to charges of pinkness, but neither of whom endorsed without qualification the Supreme Court's ruling against the white primary, the findings of Truman's Commission on Civil Rights in 1947, or Truman's civil rights package to Congress the following year. Although, like Pepper, Graham would be unseated in 1950 by a scurrilous opponent who depicted him as a race mixer as well as a communist sympathizer, as president of the University of North Carolina in 1947, Graham had proposed the creation of a segregated school of medicine.[17]

At the middle of the twentieth century when outspoken black journalist John McCray asked in his Columbia, South Carolina, weekly, *Lighthouse and Informer*, "What has the [white] South done for the Negro?" he answered his own question forthrightly and succinctly: "Nothing. Nothing they didn't have to do. Everything that has been done has been done by the Negro, or by the threat of federal court action." In fact, as Tony Badger has pointed out, the most concrete achievements in improving educational opportunities for blacks in the South came not from its moderate politicians but its staunch segregationists who, sensing a clear shift in judicial currents, had begun in the wake of World War II to support efforts to upgrade black schools in hope of making separate seem a little more equal.[18]

Perhaps the real key to understanding the limits of southern racial progress and the potential for further progress before the *Brown* decision lies not in what the conservative white majority hoped to forestall but what the liberal white minority declined to advocate. A combination of "New Deal idealism" and an ascendant "critical realism" had marked the emergence of a decidedly more liberal trend in southern thought in the 1930s and unloosed what Ralph McGill described as a "mighty surge of discussion, debate, self-examination, confession and release." This surge was not mighty enough, however, to breach or even crash heavily against the sturdy seawall of strictly enforced conformity that protected the Jim Crow system. Rather, the overwhelming majority of the white participants in these discussions in the 1930s and early 1940s insisted that the issue of race could not be understood or addressed apart from economics, politics, culture, or class.[19]

Even leaders of liberal organizations like the Southern Conference for Human Welfare insisted that the "[s]outhern Negro must be emancipated economically and politically before he can be emancipated socially." Likewise, the Southern Regional Council, organized in 1944, typified what Morton Sosna calls the "separate-but-equal liberalism" of enlightened white southerners seeking, in Numan Bartley's words, to "improve race relations within a *segregated* society through research and education, as well as through behind-the-scenes efforts to foster racial moderation among southern political and economic leaders."[20]

When the contradictions and embarrassments of the Jim Crow system were laid bare by World War II, many southern white liberals of the 1930s who still refused to renounce racial separation received what Sosna calls "a rude jolt." One of the first to be so jolted was W. T. Couch, director of the University of North Carolina Press. When he contacted African American historian Rayford W. Logan in 1943 about putting together a collection of essays organized around the theme "What the Negro Wants," Couch expected the consensus would fall close to his own view that segregation was a permanent fixture of southern life, and therefore the best course of action was to make it as nondiscriminatory as possible. The list of essayists ran the gamut from W. E. B. Du Bois on the left to F. D. Patterson, the president of Tuskegee, on the right, but upon receiving the manuscript, Couch was stunned to find even the cautious Patterson forthrightly condemning segregation as "inconsistent with the guarantees of American democracy." An angry Couch advised Logan that "[i]f this is what the Negro wants . . . nothing is clearer than what he needs and needs most urgently is to revise his wants."[21]

Trying to persuade Logan that his contributors should back off their demands for an immediate end to segregation, Couch warned that even if it were desirable, this could not possibly be achieved in less than fifty to a hundred years, much less overnight. Unable either to bring Logan around to his point of view or to wriggle out of the publication contract for the book, Couch felt compelled to add a "Publisher's Introduction" in which he essentially disavowed the arguments of the contributors and insisted that immediate desegregation would be "disastrous for everyone." Couch's response to the essays, Langston Hughes observed, was further evidence that the South's white liberals were "crowding Hitler for elbow room." In a similar allusion Sterling Brown pointed out that not all the resistance to racial change in the South came from "the demagogues and their Gestapos—the frontier thugs, the state constabularies, the goon squads, and the lynchers. . . . Many of the intellectuals speak lines that sound like Talmadge and [hate-mongering Mississippi congressman John] Rankin."[22]

Even more moderate whites like Mississippi writer David L. Cohn, who insisted repeatedly over the span of several decades that the "Southern Negro" was making great progress, "carving out for himself a worthy place in the empire of the South," also cautioned that this would continue only as long as white southerners were allowed to do the right thing at their own pace, without pressure from the North to move more quickly. Cohn believed "almost all the differences between the races may be gradually adjusted or removed through the exercise of patience, wisdom, and good will on both sides," provided northern critics would only agree that "the issue of segregation must not be called into question." Invoking William Graham Sumners's dictum that "you cannot change the mores of a people by law," Cohn described segregation as an "iron taboo" that southern whites "will not in any foreseeable time relax." In the event of any attempt to eradicate racial separation by "federal fiat," Cohn had "no doubt that every southern white man would spring to arms and the country would be swept by civil war."[23]

This was the message of long-winded lawyer Gavin Stevens, who warned in William Faulkner's 1948 novel *Intruder in the Dust* that the white southerners who "genuinely regretted the black southerners' shameful condition and would improve it" would respond to northern efforts to force the issue by moving "willy-nilly into alliance" with rabidly racist whites "with whom we have no kinship whatever in defense of a principle which we ourselves begrieve and abhor." Struggling and squirming, Faulkner himself would say much the same thing on a number of occasions, none more memorable than the interview in which he insisted that if he were forced to choose, he would "fight for Mississippi against the United States even if it meant going out into the street and shooting Negroes." Regardless of whether this dramatic and, if Faulkner is to be believed, drunken statement held true for most southern liberals, Faulkner's presumption of a violent reaction from his fellow southern whites certainly did. Like Faulkner, they generally premised their positions not on what should be done but on what they believed the mass of white southerners would accept. Because they feared that any more aggressive approach would surely force them to make the kind of agonized decision that Faulkner described, most sought what he called "a middle road," which actually led nowhere.[24]

A notable exception was Lillian Smith, whose devastating assaults on the injustice and hypocrisy of segregation and fearless explorations of the repressed guilt and sexuality that festered within the southern white psyche had taken her well beyond where most white liberals were willing to go on the race issue at the end of the 1940s. Stung by the negative reaction of Ralph McGill and others of a more moderate inclination to her brilliant but searing analysis of the Jim Crow South in *Killers of the Dream*, Smith complained in 1949 that "75 percent of the 'liberals' in the South seem to favor segregation." She exaggerated but little. When the Southern Regional Council finally went on record that year as being officially opposed to segregation, the fallout was evident in the shrinkage of its membership base from thirty-four hundred in 1950 to eighteen hundred four years later. If the South on the eve of the *Brown* decision was in the middle of Klarman's meaningful "indigenous racial transformation," it was proceeding without the participation or endorsement of the majority of the region's ostensibly most enlightened whites.[25]

What caused southern white liberals "to temporize and waver on issues involving Negro rights," Junius Scales observed, "was the vested interest and depth, scope and sheer virulence of the bigotry they opposed." In reality, however, it was not simply the prospect of physical or verbal abuse but the threat of isolation and loss of community that hamstrung white liberals in the South. Robert Penn Warren described this apprehension when he admitted that when he had seen a white man beating a black teenager in Baton Rouge in 1939, he had been temporarily immobilized, not by "simple cowardice" but by a "sudden, appalling sense of aloneness," a "paralyzing sense of being outside my own community."[26]

For all the ways that segregation and racial discrimination clearly contradicted the Christian doctrine that reverberated from the pulpits of the Bible Belt South, for southern whites the community of faith and the community of race were essentially one and the same. When a young Greenville, Mississippi, man's belief that his church should accept black worshipers put him at odds with his mother, he asked her pointedly, "What do you think Jesus Christ would do if He were standing at the front door of the First Presbyterian Church?" "I know exactly what he would do," the mother responded, "and he would be wrong." Although they had trouble refuting the assertion that blacks and whites would be together in heaven, southern whites clearly preferred to wait until then.[27]

Whites who stepped outside their racial community often put their own or their family's social or economic standing in jeopardy. Montgomery attorney Clifford Durr's willingness to take on the cases of indigent blacks clearly cost him a number of white clients. Durr's wife, Virginia, noted that the black children involved in the early integration of the local schools were seen as intruders by their white schoolmates but hailed as heroes within their own communities, while the Durr children, owing to the racial liberalism of their parents, were "pariahs and outcasts" among their peers. It was by no means necessary to challenge the entire system openly and directly. Even the slightest variation from the prescribed norm might mean rejection even by one's inner circle. When a young black man enrolled in the Law School at the University of Virginia in 1950, Sarah Patton Boyle sent him a simple welcome note, only to find that she had made herself persona non grata among the other faculty wives.[28]

I witnessed first hand the pressure for racial conformity that still prevailed among white southerners in the 1950s. Like many guilt-ridden white liberals of my generation, I feel somehow constrained to point out that I was raised in a home where I was forbidden to use the "n-word." Although my father rarely used the term in talking with me or my mother, I noticed that he was more likely to employ it when he was among a group of his male friends. When I was about twelve, my father received a call telling him that Wyatt Mattox, a black man who lived in a house on our property, had been found dead in his kitchen. Wyatt worked as an orderly at the local hospital, and he had helped to bathe and care for my grandfather during his terminal illness. Daddy had constantly praised Wyatt and his wife for their responsibility and intelligence, and he was clearly upset by Wyatt's death. Yet, when he phoned the sheriff to notify him that Wyatt's body had been found, he began by saying, almost matter-of-factly, "Sheriff, I got a dead nigger out here." Within the confines of our family circle Wyatt's color had not prevented him from being seen as a fine person, but when it came time to refer to him in conversation with another white man, my father had simply reduced him to "a dead nigger." Only years later did I understand that here, from my own flesh and blood, was flesh and blood validation of Ralph Ellison's brilliant novel, *Invisible Man,* whose naive young black protagonist quickly learns that despite his uncommon intelligence and accomplishment, he is invisible to whites as anything more than just another black man marked by all the negative traits they have ascribed to his entire race.

Even after segregation's barriers had been breached, the pervasive coercions of the Jim Crow mind-set proved again and again that individuals are more moral than groups. Pat Watters related an encounter that seems in its own way as cruel, shameful, and tragic as any of the bloody and brutal events that made headlines during the confrontational stages of the civil rights movement. A white teacher, considered "liberal" by the standards of her Black Belt community, had but one African American student in her newly integrated second-grade class. As was her custom, on the last day of school she had her class file by her desk for a hug and the requisite good-byes. "And do you know," she explained in a surprised tone, "that little colored boy came, too, holding his arms out to me like the rest. And I just had to push him away. All the other children were there watching. I just had to. Can you imagine him doing that?" Even after integration and before an audience consisting only of seven- and eight-year-olds, this white teacher demonstrated what Watters called "a compartmentalizing ability to shut out from consciousness the sad and the evil . . . to make unreal anything that we were unwilling to mention."[29]

The shelves in our libraries groan with weighty tomes dedicated to unraveling the complex braid of emotional and psychological factors that continued, even at the middle of the twentieth century, to bind white southerners to the Jim Crow system. Before we simply attribute this enduring pattern of racial behavior to ignorance, irrationality, or some sort of social and cultural inertia, it is important to recall Barrington Moore's warning that to do so is "to overlook the concrete interests and privileges that are served by . . . the entire complicated process of transmitting culture from one generation to the next."

In a rigidly white supremacist society, the perks of prejudice and discrimination were often too substantial and seductive for even the thoughtful and sensitive white southerner to resist. Black domestic and farm labor was still relatively cheap and pliable, and the sense of power, status, and self-esteem derived from living among those deemed inferior to you could be absolutely intoxicating. Reflecting on his youth in Yazoo City, Mississippi, in the 1940s and early 1950s, Willie Morris recalled that he had once dreamed of an uncomplicated life of emotional and physical comfort as a "member of Mississippi's educated landed gentry," married to a lovely Delta plantation belle, and presiding over "Boll weevils big enough to wear dog tags, pre–Earl Warren darkies, and the young squirearchy from plantations abutting on Carter, Eden, Holly Bluff, Sidon and Tchula."[30]

Morris confessed that his attitude and behavior toward black people had ranged from "a kind of unconscious affection, touched with a sense of excitement and sometimes pity," to "sudden emotional eruptions — of disdain and utter cruelty." Though he had felt temporary pangs of guilt, he seldom questioned his "alternating affections and cruelties" toward African Americans because the feeling that blacks in Yazoo were "ours to do with as we wished" like "some tangible possession" had been "rooted so deeply in me by the whole moral atmosphere of the place."[31]

The South of the 1950s was definitely an improvement over the South of the 1880s. Still, the man who told a young Melton McLaurin that "you can educate a nigger all you want . . . but he's still just a nigger" was hardly less representative of dominant white attitudes in mid-1950s North Carolina than the white teacher in Mississippi who, twenty years earlier, had assured Hortense Powdermaker that no matter how much education a black person received, "a million years from now, a nigger will still be a nigger in the South." Likewise, what Powdermaker saw in the mid-1930s as "the special inducements to inertia" were still significant enough that the overwhelming majority of white southerners were less likely to condemn the evils of the status quo than simply continue to "consider them inevitable."[32]

Critical minimizers of *Brown*'s significance have exaggerated not only the extent of southern racial progress in the post–World War II decade but the mounting pressure for racial change from outside the South as well. For example, Gerald Rosenberg argues that a number of factors, ranging from the Cold War to growing black political influence in the North to "the increase in mass communication," actually "created the pressure that led to civil rights. The Court reflected that pressure; it did not create it." In effect, Klarman and others who cite *Brown* as proof that Supreme Court decrees "rarely deviate far from dominant public opinion" essentially put the *Brown* court in the same boat with the *Plessy* court it was trying to overturn. There is little difference, after all, in arguing that the justices had simply bowed to "entrenched social mores" in the South and militant white indifference in the North when they upheld segregation in 1896 than in arguing (apparently on the rather shaky basis of a poll taken *after* the *Brown* decision was announced) the justices were merely reflecting the views of "roughly half the country" when they moved to strike it down in 1954.[33]

Certainly, the familiar maxim that the Supreme Court follows the election returns does not seem to apply here. Two years before *Brown* neither party had exactly made civil rights a priority in its push for the White House, and enough southern whites had felt so confident of the GOP nominee's indifference to the issue that five southern states had fallen into Republican hands. Rosenberg insists that the *Brown* court was merely caught up in a historical current "but contributed little to it." Yet surveys indicated at the time that only a negligible percentage of Americans thought civil rights was the nation's most serious problem. Moreover, the absence of anything resembling a groundswell of support outside the South for strict and speedy enforcement of the *Brown* decree suggests that the Court had far more assurance of a positive response from northern whites when it validated segregation in 1896 than when it struck it down in 1954. Regardless of how skillfully the Court's intentions may be spun, the preponderance of the evidence indicates to me that the *Brown* decision represented an attempt to take one segment of the nation's population not just further than it wanted to go but further than the majority of the remaining population wanted to force it to go at the time.[34]

Even the most casual student of the civil rights movement understands that dramatic, widespread progress toward making racial integration a reality throughout southern and American life did not come until black activists took to the streets and lunch counters to demand it. To suggest that *Brown* did not help to inspire such activism, however, is, as David J. Garrow points out, to dismiss Rosa Parks's observation that, because of *Brown*, "African-Americans believed that at last there was a real chance to change the segregation laws" and to ignore Martin Luther King Jr.'s judgment in 1958 that the ruling had "brought hope to millions of disinherited Negroes who had formerly dared only to dream of freedom."[35]

Those who minimize the *Brown* decision's role in encouraging civil rights activism also largely ignore the hundreds of African Americans who, in the months after the ruling, incurred the wrath of local whites in at least sixty southern communities by petitioning for immediate school integration. *Brown* critics insist on seeing this wrath, embodied in the growth of the Citizens Council in the Deep South and the rise of the "massive resistance" movement regionwide, as simply part of a white backlash against the Court's decree, rather than an outraged response to actions inspired by that decree.

Several critical commentators have observed that the reaction of southern whites to the first *Brown* decision in May 1954 was actually relatively muted compared to the vociferously defiant response to the second *Brown* ruling that came slightly more than a year later and, instead of setting specific goals and deadlines, simply ordered that school desegregation be accomplished "with all deliberate speed." This apparent concession to the recalcitrance of southern whites may have actually reinforced that recalcitrance by giving segregationists reason to doubt the Court's resolve and believe that its ruling could be resisted successfully. Here again, however, it is difficult to separate white anger at the Court from white anger at black activists whose behavior demonstrated, contrary to segregationist claims, that African Americans not only wanted integration but wanted it right then. These efforts included not just the local desegregation petitions and the Montgomery bus boycott but the enrollment of Autherine Lucy at the University of Alabama in February 1956, which served as the immediate backdrop for the "Southern Manifesto" of segregationist defiance endorsed by the overwhelming majority of the region's representatives in the House and Senate. In short, there is good reason to believe that much of what Klarman calls "post-*Brown* [white] racial fanaticism" was actually induced by post-*Brown* black aggressiveness instead. If later protests were not a direct response to *Brown,* they were surely a reaction at least in part to the increasingly inescapable conclusion that white southerners clearly had no intention of accepting any sort of integration voluntarily and that Washington was in no great hurry to force them.[36]

Despite suggestions that the *Brown* decision's greatest contribution to the civil rights movement came not in inspiring protests but in encouraging the violent southern white reactions to them that ultimately prodded Congress into passing the landmark civil rights legislation of the mid-1960s, there is simply no basis for concluding that white southerners' response to such protests would have been significantly less hostile without *Brown*. Klarman insists that if *Brown* had never happened, he can "imagine Freedom Riders arriving in Birmingham and Montgomery without police commissioners inviting Klansmen to beat them, and . . . blacks demonstrating for voting rights in Selma without law enforcement officers brutalizing them." So can I, I suppose, provided we're talking about the 1980s instead of the 1960s and assuming that these things would have happened at all without *Brown*.[37]

The "down-on-*Brown*" crowd seems inordinately fond of "might haves." Gerald Rosenberg has suggested that, even without *Brown*, by the late 1960s the threat of withholding federal funds might have led southern school boards to challenge their state's segregation laws. Elsewhere, upset by the sorry contemporary state of too many still predominantly black schools, Derrick Bell has argued that the cause of black education might have been better served had the justices simply concluded in 1954 that overturning *Plessy v. Ferguson* was less important than providing "the educational equity long denied under the separate but equal rhetoric." Accordingly, in Bell's imagined alternative, the Court would have established a judicially monitored process giving southern school districts three years both to equalize school expenditures across racial lines and to bring them in line with a nationwide academic norm for "school systems of comparable size and resources." School boards unwilling or unable to meet this standard would face an order for immediate integration.[38]

Bell's "integrate-or-equalize" approach might have benefited some black institutions in urban areas where affluent whites were willing to pony up to avoid sending their kids to racially mixed schools. However, because the greatest racial disparities in school expenditures were in the impoverished rural systems that could least afford to remedy them, in Bell's scenario the first white schools forced to desegregate would have been those likely to resist it most ferociously. Beyond that, so long as southern federal judges were part of the monitoring process, any "integrate-or-equalize" plan surely would have faced just as much, if not more, of the obstructionism encountered by the actual *Brown* decree. Therefore, as with the real *Brown* decision, the political pressure needed to make separate but equal truly equal would likely still have required the kinds of black protests and violent white responses that were needed to get congressional action on the Civil Rights Act of 1964 and the Voting Rights Act of 1965.

C. Vann Woodward's *The Strange Career of Jim Crow* demonstrated that, even though the supporting evidence is scant, persuasive suggestions about an alternative past can make it easier for readers to conceive of an alternative present. In his case, however, the need for a new present was both clear and compelling, and the suggestions themselves were at least cautious and qualified. Even so, Woodward admitted that his imaginative effort to convince readers that Jim Crow was neither inevitable nor invincible might have led some readers to see him as a pushover. This should remind us that, regardless of one's intentions, the consequences of trying to interpret what is happening today on the basis of a counterfactual revision of yesterday can never be fully anticipated, much less controlled.

It is surely more than coincidence that the chorus of criticism aimed at the *Brown* decision has emerged almost in tandem with a similar argument that the abortion rights movement might have fared better had the Court been less forceful in its ruling in *Roe v. Wade* in 1973. Meanwhile, the increasingly narrow ideological parameters applied to the selection and confirmation of federal judges has fueled not only apprehension about "activist judges" at both ends of the political spectrum but a concomitant skepticism of the very principle of judicial review itself.

This is not the first time that the *Brown* decision has been used to buttress criticism of judicial review. In a decidedly disapproving 1984 exploration, *The Burden of Brown*, conservative historian Raymond Wolters Jr. lauded the whites of Prince Edward County, Virginia, who closed their schools rather than abide by the Court's decree, and insisted that "in a democracy social reform should be undertaken by the people's elected representatives, not by unethical judges." One prominent contemporary critic of judicial review is none other than conservative Supreme Court justice Antonin Scalia, but owing perhaps to the Court's recent rightward tilt, which Scalia represents, much of the current storm seems to be blowing in from the left. Liberal scholar Mark Tushnet sounded much like Wolters and Scalia when he advocated "taking the Constitution away from the courts" by substituting legislative or political constitutionalism for our traditional reliance on the judiciary. To this end, Tushnet has even floated the idea of a constitutional amendment that would deny the Supreme Court's authority to determine the constitutionality of congressional legislation.[39]

Suffice it to say, such a move would raise an entirely new set of concerns by supplanting the Court's inherent gradualism with the inherent ephemerality of a legislative process that operates without the constraints of legal precedent or principle. Because what is enacted in one congressional session may simply be abolished in the next, there would be little of the continuity that the very concept of the protection of rights implies. Tushnet may be correct in suggesting that *Brown* was not "a strong demonstration of how the court can bring about change on behalf of those who lack political power."

One might counter, of course, that with but few exceptions, the same might be said of congressional responses to black concerns from the end of the first Reconstruction until the second one had already garnered widespread white support.[40]

There is a malicious rumor afloat that our Washington lawmakers may sometimes be more responsive to powerful and moneyed special interests than to the views of their constituents at large. Moreover, would we really want to entrust primary constitutional authority to the same body that responded to the post-9/11 panic by tossing certain fundamental guarantees of due process and free speech out the window? Surely, if we are to think more than twice about stripping or curtailing the Court's exercise of judicial review, we should have a lot more to go on than the flimsy, illogical, and essentially ahistorical case that the revisionist critics of *Brown* have served up. Otherwise, as I am sure that great legal scholar Jimmy Buffett would agree, we might learn the hard way that, as a "permanent reminder of a temporary feeling," a constitutional amendment is far more problematic than a tattoo.[41]

Having graduated from an all-white high school eleven years after the Supreme Court declared all-white schools unconstitutional, I am well aware that its decree was hardly a fast-acting remedy for racial injustice, and clearly, by itself, it was far from a perfect or complete one, either. Even today, as your grown-up, garden-variety guilty white southerner, I can find plenty of evidence of *Brown*'s limitations, especially each spring when, in some communities, privately organized, racially separate high school proms remain the order of the day.

However, a great many, if not most, of the recent negative appraisals of racial progress since *Brown* focus on problems well above the Mason-Dixon line, and I suspect that disappointment with the legacy of *Brown v. Board of Education* is really a reflection of a larger national malaise on issues of race. By opening the way to addressing a single region's racial injustices, the *Brown* court actually set in motion a process that led ultimately to the sobering acknowledgment that racism was not simply a regional affliction but a national one. Things certainly seemed a lot less complicated back in 1954, when practically the only whites who were talking about racial problems outside the South were southerners trying to deflect criticism from themselves. Although some critics of the *Brown* decision are reluctant to credit it for energizing the civil rights movement, they are not at all hesitant to effectively blame a ruling that simply ordered an end to de jure racial segregation in the public schools for all the perceived underachievements of the larger, almost parameter-less, crusade for racial equality in all aspects of American life. Thus Derrick Bell holds *Brown* accountable for today's "ever-widening racial disparities," and Charles Ogletree describes everything from the precarious position of many historically black colleges and universities and the decay of other black cultural institutions to the demise of affirmative action as "current manifestations of *Brown*'s failures."[42]

The insistence on seeing *Brown*'s glass as half empty rather than half full probably stems in part from a legitimate concern that too starry an assessment of the gains of the last half-century will make "We Shall Overcome" a purely historical anthem when it still retains so much contemporary relevance. Still, the consistent contemporary emphasis on what either the *Brown* decision or, for that matter, the civil rights movement failed to accomplish in an arbitrarily imposed span of fifty years suggests a certain loss of perspective. Before we are totally enveloped in debilitating gloom, we might do well to Google the nooks and crannies of history for more successful efforts to facilitate mutual acceptance between two distinct racial groups, living contiguously and struggling to overcome nearly four centuries' worth of a common but bitterly divisive past in which one had been enslaved and then summarily resubjugated by the other.

Surprisingly enough, anyone wishing to accentuate *Brown*'s positives is likely to point to the society that once resisted it most aggressively. Although the South is still far from a picture postcard of racial harmony, there is no escaping the reality that in the half-century since this momentous ruling, the South has become the nation's most residentially, educationally, and politically integrated region and the destination of choice for relocating African Americans. Once a place for blacks to flee, it is now a place to come back to and call home.

Many factors contributed to this outcome, not the least being the courage of those who took to the streets to press the *Brown* decision's case against Jim Crow. Those who argue that some sort of "racial reform" was inevitable, regardless of how the Court had ruled on May 17, 1954, may well be correct, but the effectiveness of their critical and dismissive treatments of *Brown* derives not from the strength of their cases for what could have happened *without* it but from widespread disappointment with what actually happened *with* it. Although contemporary liberals might not appreciate the analogy, one need only consider the tragic consequences of so many white southerners' obsession with refighting the Civil War to understand that succumbing to the seductive fantasy of what "might have been" can seriously undermine our efforts to make a reality of what "ought to be."

3 *Brown* and Belonging

African Americans and the Recovery of Southern Black Identity

A decade before the 1954 *Brown v. Board of Education* decision invalidated racial segregation in the public schools, writer Sterling Brown began his contribution to the controversial volume *What the Negro Wants* by citing a recently published history of Georgia whose white author took great comfort in the fact that the "Anglo-Saxon . . . race makes up nearly one hundred percent of the population of the South." Brown attributed the apparent invisibility of more than one-third of the state's inhabitants to the propensity of whites to see "only the people that count." In the stage play that was the Jim Crow South, he seemed to be saying, blacks were not actors so much as part of the set, discernible only as a distant, undifferentiated forest rather than up close, as individual trees.[1]

Brown's point was not lost on his friend and protégé of sorts, Ralph Ellison, whose protagonist in the 1952 novel *Invisible Man* encountered the first evidence of his own invisibility in the South's tightly woven fabric of custom and law that smothered individual black personalities under a thick blanket of racial stereotypes. A few years earlier Richard Wright's semiautobiographical *Black Boy* had shown how these stereotypes were used, in turn, to support the dogma of caste that had imposed them in the first place. As a young man, Wright had actually made whites uneasy and suspicious with his refusal to steal, and thereby affirm the congenital moral weakness of his race. Whites also noticed his reluctance to "laugh and talk" with other blacks in the happy-go-lucky manner that supposedly demonstrated their fundamental contentment with their lot in the Jim Crow South.

Not only had the southern whites who claimed they "knew 'niggers.' . . . not known me," Wright insisted, but by pressuring him to be "what the whites had said that I must be," they had prevented him from really knowing "who I was" as well. Accordingly, he had left the South after realizing that its white racist mentality "could recognize but part of a man, could accept but a fragment of his personality and all the rest—the best and deepest things of heart and mind—were tossed away in blind ignorance and hate."[2]

Reflecting these sentiments in a very emotional way, two days after the *Brown* decision came down, Ralph Ellison wrote his former mentor at Tuskegee, rejoicing that "the court has found in our favor and recognized our human psychological complexity and citizenship and another battle of the Civil War has been won." Though acutely aware of "the problems that lie ahead," Ellison found it "hopeful and good" that "the judges have found and Negroes must be individuals. . . . [H]ere's to integration, the only integration that counts: that of the personality."[3]

Here, then, was the message that black writers had been sending for decades. "Negroes want to be counted in. They want to belong," as Sterling Brown had put it in 1944, and "however segregation may be rationalized, it is essentially the denial of belonging." Critics charged that the *Brown* decision was grounded in sociological theory rather than actual legal precedent. However, the *Brown* court's finding, that setting black schoolchildren apart "solely because of their race . . . may affect their hearts and minds in a way unlikely ever to be undone," revealed remarkable empathy for those whose "belonging" had been denied. As Eric J. Sundquist has explained, in *Brown* the Court made integrated education the means by which African Americans would finally achieve the end of "valued and meaningful membership in the nation."[4]

Most contemporary liberal observers assumed that blacks cared only about belonging as Americans and not as southerners as well. Focusing on the suffering imposed by the southern racial system, external critics found it logical to conclude that the last thing that any black person would crave would be an identification with the South. Most who rejected white southerners' protestations that the blacks who faced constant abuse and exploitation in the Jim Crow South were nonetheless contented and carefree simply embraced the counterfallacy that all African Americans must be totally and eternally estranged from a place where they had endured so much injustice and hardship. Recognition that black southerners could have emotional ties to the South also ran counter to the emerging black power/black pride movements of the 1960s, which focused on the roots of black identity in the African homeland, rather than in the slave South where Africans had been dragged against their will and subjected to brutal, dehumanizing treatment at the hands of their white oppressors. As Ralph Ellison observed in 1965, "Love of the South is glamorized by the white Southerner; but the idea that a Negro may love the South is usually denied as an utterly outrageous idea."[5]

Viewed against this backdrop, perhaps no cultural phenomenon of the post-civil-rights era proved more striking than the readiness, even eagerness, of many African Americans, both in the South and outside it, to identify themselves unequivocally as southerners and to claim the region as home. Survey data from 1964–76 reveal significant changes in the sentiments of both southern and non-southern blacks. In 1964 only 55 percent of southern black respondents expressed "warm" feelings toward southerners, as opposed to the nearly 90 percent of southern whites who gave this response. By 1976, however, the proportion of southern blacks who registered this warmth stood at nearly 80 percent and only slightly below the percentage of white southerners who felt that way. Analyzing this data, John Shelton Reed and Merle Black have concluded that in 1964 "many Southern blacks may have been unclear about whether the category ["southerners"] was meant to include them and their black friends and neighbors. . . . By the 1970s, it appears, many southern blacks did understand themselves to be southerners, and they were not unhappy about it." Throughout the 1980s and 1990s similar polls produced similar results, and by 2001 the percentage of blacks in the South who identified themselves as southerners was actually slightly higher than that for whites.[6]

Evidence of this trend was not confined merely to opinion surveys. Peter Applebome was surely correct in 1994 when he wrote that "in a logical extension of the civil rights battles of the past, [blacks] are staking claim to their vision of the South—not as background figures on the mythic landscape of moonlight and magnolias, not as victims of oppression dragged here from Africa, but as southerners, with as much stake in the region as any Mississippi planter or Virginia farmer." As historian John Hope Franklin has explained, "The South as a place is as attractive to blacks as it is to whites. . . . Blacks even when they left the South didn't stop having affection for it. They just couldn't make it there." Veteran African American journalist Fred Powledge could not recall ever hearing a black person in the South object to being called a southerner. Writing in 1979, Powledge insisted, "Black people *are* Southerners. They are of and by and from and for the South at least as much as their white brethren, and many have repeatedly demonstrated . . . their love for and faith in the region."[7]

Novelist Alice Walker has credited the Reverend Martin Luther King Jr. with inspiring her to resist the Jim Crow forces that had worked to "disinherit" her and to vow that she would "never be forced away from the land of my birth without a fight." In her 1972 tribute to King, she thanked him for leading this fight: "He gave us back our heritage. He gave us back our homeland. . . . He gave us continuity of place, without which community is ephemeral. He gave us home." Actor Morgan Freeman said much the same thing some thirty years later. Relishing the irony of the South's role as "the new comfort zone" for so many blacks, Freeman insisted, "If Dr. King were back and he were told that, I think he'd believe it.

Of course he would. That's what he meant to happen, that the South would be a place that we don't have to run away from. As a matter of fact, we want to run home."[8]

Demographic data clearly confirm this impression. Between 1910 and 1960, nearly 10 million blacks left the South, but in the 1970s the region began to show net gains through black migration. This trend continued throughout the 1980s and accelerated dramatically in the 1990s. During the last quarter of the twentieth century, the number of African Americans entering the region exceeded the number leaving by more than 1.2 million. During the 1990s alone the South's black population grew by nearly 3.6 million overall, nearly twice the rate of increase for the previous decade.[9]

African American literary scholar Thadious M. Davis has observed that "while anthropologists and sociologists may see the increasingly frequent pattern of black return migration [to the South] as flight from the hardships of urban life, I would suggest that it is also a laying claim to a culture and to a region that, though fraught with pain and difficulty, provides a major grounding for identity." When forced to confront the nature of their own feelings about the South, blacks in the region had historically presented what L. D. Reddick called "a study in attachment and alienation," alternately expressing their "love and hate" and finding themselves struggling with "a great and confusing frustration." John Hope Franklin's research on runaway slaves has revealed that "though blacks, with few exceptions, rejected slavery, they did not reject the land or the region." Celebrated fugitive slave Frederick Douglass said as much, predicting that if emancipation came, "you would see many old and familiar faces back again to [sic] the South." Douglass may have spoken not just for those who had fled slavery but for many who had subsequently fled Jim Crow when he explained, "We want to live in the land of our birth and to lay our bones by the side of our fathers; nothing short of an intense love of personal freedom keeps us from the South."[10]

With the Great Migration of black people out of the region in full swing by the 1920s, many African Americans proclaimed that they would rather "be a lamp post in Harlem, than the mayor of Atlanta." Much as the civil rights movement would do for a later generation of black writers, however, the move to the North freed some key participants in the Harlem Renaissance from the South's constant emotional pressures and stifling intellectual restraints and allowed them to look with greater detachment at a society and culture that, for better or worse, had helped to make them who they were. For all his feelings of estrangement, as he headed north in 1927 even Richard Wright had realized "deep down . . . that I could never really leave the South, for my feelings had already been formed by the South, for there had been slowly instilled into my personality and consciousness, black though I was, the culture of the South."[11]

Although he wrote of its racial horrors, Langston Hughes also fantasized in 1922 about "the magnolia-scented South, / Beautiful like a woman, seductive as a dark-eyed whore" and complained that "I am who am black, would love her" and "give her many rare gifts," but "she spits in my face" and "turns her back on me." Surveying the short fiction produced by Hughes and other writers of the Harlem Renaissance, Robert Bone found a "deep affection for the rural South, despite the terror and brutality which all too often were visited upon him within its precincts." Randall Kenan seemed to affirm this ambivalence for post-civil-rights-era southern black writers, who, he believed, walked "a fine line, something between revulsion and acceptance . . . so often reflecting about wanting to get out of the South, but at the same time knowing . . . that this is what sustains you, this is what makes you who you are."[12]

Commenting on the assumption that blacks would be hopelessly alienated from a setting where they had suffered so much, Ralph Ellison understood why "it is hard to contemplate an elasticity which allows us to survive the total efforts at brutalization during various periods and still to affirm the seasons, the landscape, the birds and so on." Maya Angelou clearly felt a strong personal attachment to the South as both a place and a source of identity, confessing "sympathy for black people who have no southern roots." Alice Walker also expressed regret for her "Northern brothers" because "in the cities, it cannot be so clear to one that he is a creature of the earth, feeling the soil between the toes, smelling the dust thrown up by the rain, loving the earth so much that one longs to taste it and sometimes does."[13]

Nikki Giovanni seemed to speak directly to Sterling Brown's concerns when she asserted that Knoxville is "a place where no matter what, I belong" and that in turn "Knoxville belongs to me." Determined that her son also "must know we come from somewhere. That we belong," Giovanni reflected in her autobiographical *Gemini* on her youthful experiences in Knoxville and her grandparents' neighborhood, which was later destroyed by urban renewal. She mused poetically that white biographers would "probably talk about my hard childhood / and never understand that / all the while I was quite happy." Giovanni addressed this possibility in *Knoxville, Tennessee,* a beautifully illustrated children's book recalling the pleasures of fresh vegetables, barbecue, buttermilk, church socials, and mountain picnics with her grandmother. Such emotions seem strikingly reminiscent of the words of Harlem Renaissance writers like Sterling Brown, Jean Toomer, and Langston Hughes, all of whom alluded to the beauty and sensory pull of the South.[14]

If, in the post-civil-rights Sun Belt era, white writers like Walker Percy could shift their attention from the struggle with the South's backwardness to the struggle with its ostensible "progress," black writers could redirect their focus as well. Specifically, they could look beyond the painful effects of slavery and Jim Crow to examine southern black life as not just a desperate struggle against victimization and oppression but the story of individual people who came equipped with flaws as well as virtues and managed not only to find joy and satisfaction in their own lives but sometimes to inflict worry and pain on the lives of others. The pressures to present a united front during the activist phase of the civil rights movement would have made such a novel most unlikely during the 1960s, but Alice Walker's *The Color Purple* (1982) represented a dramatic break-through in the treatment of southern black life by black writers themselves. In both its critical perspective on male-female interaction and its more affirmative treatment of the supportive bonds among black women, it reflected not only the influences of the women's liberation movement but the accomplishments of a civil rights crusade that, whatever its shortcomings, nonetheless gave black writers the opportunity to treat their own culture and community with greater candor and critical insight.[15]

South Carolina novelist Dori Sanders was particularly forthright when she insisted, "I am a southern writer and felt in advance I'd be seen that way . . . such a richness of place! How could someone grow up in the South and not aspire to be a writer?" Likewise, asked whether he objected to being labeled a "southern black writer," Randall Kenan responded, "I was born in North Carolina and my skin is the color of coffee without cream. To me it's silly to assume that I can be anything other than a Southern, black writer." Such comments should not have been surprising. Unlike many of their white counterparts, who were struggling to come to grips with what they saw as a contemporary South that had largely lost its historic distinctiveness, as Frank Shelton suggested in 1994, southern black writers were still pursuing "the meaning of life . . . through forging a personal connection with Southern history." Though it is burdened by "enslavement, prejudice and racism," this history gave them the strength derived from "a relationship with the land and a place in a community of people nurtured by a pastoral environment."[16]

In fact, by the 1990s, as Fred Hobson has observed, the black writer might actually be seen as "the quintessential Southern writer—with his emphasis on family and community, his essentially concrete vision, his feeling for place, his legacy of failure, poverty, defeat, and those other well-known qualities of the Southern experience, his immersion in history and what it produced." To Hobson, "any writer with those qualities and that legacy would seem to be, in many respects, the truest contemporary heir to the Southern literary tradition."[17]

The emergence of African American writers as the most identifiably southern literary figures of the late twentieth century struck Hobson as "a final irony of Southern history." In reality, however, other but related ironies lay close at hand. Writing in 1970, when the echoes of the civil rights crusade had scarcely died away, Alice Walker exulted that "what the black Southern writer inherits as a natural right is a sense of community." The hard-won advances of the 1950s and 1960s freed many African Americans to embrace their southern roots and celebrate and examine their attachments to southern people and places. For some, however, the long-awaited, much-suffered-for destruction of Jim Crow, with its barriers to educational, social, and economic advancement, actually seemed in the long run to erode this cherished sense of solidarity and belonging.[18]

As the last generation of black southerners who grew up under segregation approached middle age, some were even expressing a distinctive sense of nostalgia and loss when they looked back on their experiences in the segregated South. Born and raised in Glen Allan, Mississippi, and gone on to a successful business career, Clifton Taulbert admitted that "[e]ven though segregation was a painful reality for us, there were some very good things that happened. Today I enjoy the broader society in which I live, and I would never want to return to forced segregation, but I also have a deeply-felt sense that important values were conveyed to me in my colored childhood, values we're in danger of losing in our integrated world."[19]

Some black southerners actually associated integration with a loss of "spiritual backbone" in the black community. Reflecting on her experience at all-black Williston High School in Wilmington, North Carolina, Linda Pearce recalled that "we were in a cocoon bathed in a warm fluid, where we were expected to excel . . . and then something called desegregation punctured it. We went from our own land to being tourists in someone else's. It never did come together, and I think it's on the verge of falling apart altogether now."[20]

Betty Jo Hayes had similar feelings about her student experience at Tampa's all-black Middleton High, where "we were indeed a family. We were embraced by teachers, protected, taught everything that they thought we would need to get out there and improve the world as such. . . . We were a proud, proud, proud group." When integration came and Middleton was closed, Hayes recalled, it was "as if death had come to a community." In his elegant memoir, *Colored People*, Henry Louis Gates Jr. also told the story of his youth in the paper mill town of Piedmont, West Virginia, and conveyed his genuine sense of loss as "the last wave of the civil rights era finally came . . . crashing down on the colored world of Piedmont."[21]

In reality, the sense of lost community among many African Americans who had lived in the South before and after Jim Crow merely confirmed that black southerners had managed to retain a viable culture and a sense of their own worth in a society where color barriers had confronted them at every turn. By the end of the twentieth century, they seemed to reflect so wistfully on this accomplishment precisely because they felt increasingly hard-pressed to sustain it in a post–Jim Crow era where color counted for less but, apparently, so did family, religion, community, and other affirmative institutions that had helped to unite them in the face of oppression and restriction.

This reaction seems comparable in a sense to the way some residents of the old Soviet bloc now appear to regard their former existence, however restricted and austere, behind the iron curtain. One of the most successful films ever made in Germany, the award-winning *Goodbye Lenin*, quickly attracted more than two million viewers by reminding them that before the collapse of the Berlin Wall, East Germans had maintained their own "very normal

German world," despite the efforts of a totalitarian regime to regulate their lives and restrict their thoughts.[22]

Observing that the "nostalgic" narrative of segregation had gained "nearly universal status in black public discourse" in the 1990s, a skeptical Adolph Reed Jr. suggested that such rosy recollections of the good old days when times were bad actually represented the self-congratulatory gloating of those who believed that their superior talent and effort had enabled them to surmount the same obstacles that seemed to stop other African Americans cold. The major contributors to the "burgeoning black memoir industry" did seem to share a middle-class upbringing as the children or wards of "community notables and elites" who were often able to insulate them from the most brutal aspects of the Jim Crow system. Nationwide, the growth in the ratio between the mean incomes of the top 20 percent of black families and the bottom 20 percent exceeded that for whites by 21 percent between 1966 and 2001. Rather than smugness, however, the longing among those at the top for a time when all who were "colored" were supposedly united in the face of a common oppression more likely reflected genuine feelings of guilt or regret about the increasing social and economic distance among African Americans.[23]

Those who seemed nostalgic about the Jim Crow era actually yearned not for the days of racial separation but for what Walker called "the solidarity and sharing a modest existence can sometimes bring." Another African American observer drew a sharp distinction between "nostalgia for segregation itself" and hunger for the sense of community cohesiveness that segregation inadvertently helped to foster "before the expanded opportunities and choices in housing, jobs, and schools" secured by the civil rights movement "tended to separate us, particularly by class." Before integration strong black communities had been common throughout the South, Randall Kenan explained. The destruction of these communities was "a necessary evil," but by the end of the twentieth century, he saw black people tending to "idealize them" at least in part because "you had black doctors living next door to black postal workers." In black neighborhoods at large, with integration and enhanced mobility, residents moved up and out in increasing numbers, and once-thriving black enterprises struggled to remain competitive in a desegregated marketplace. Returning to Clarksdale, Mississippi, after a thirty-year absence, Helen O'Neal-McCray was shocked by the boarded-up black businesses and the signs of community and individual deterioration and decay. "Black people used to live all together," she lamented, "shacks and nice houses. . . . Now they're divided."[24]

Concern about the loss of racial cohesiveness clearly intensified as it became apparent that growing numbers of the black migrants to the South were upper-middle-class professionals who settled in racially diverse suburbs beyond the economic reach of most other African Americans. Racism and racial tensions were hardly on the verge of extinction, but in the suburban South, emerging evidence of new affinities based on class as well as race suggested further erosion of a sense of community among southern blacks. The number of black homeowners nearly doubled in Atlanta during the 1990s. In the 2002 Democratic primary in metro Atlanta's fourth congressional district, more economically secure black voters joined whites in supporting Denise Majette, a more conservative African American challenger who ousted maverick liberal incumbent Cynthia McKinney despite McKinney's strong base among lower-income black constituents.[25]

That such a development seems particularly noteworthy is actually more of a commentary on what was expected of the civil rights movement than what it has produced. Many black and white liberals assumed that removing racial constraints on opportunity would somehow produce an unending stream of Alice Walkers but never a Condoleezza Rice. Only recently have they begun to realize, to their dismay, that because progress did not come for all African

Americans at the same time, some of those who enjoyed the first fruits of that progress might no longer have as much in common with those who did not.

As a concerned Henry Louis Gates explained, "Precisely because of the gains we made through the civil rights movement and affirmative action, we have two distinct classes in black America, and unless we do something drastic, never the twain will meet between those two classes. Martin Luther King didn't die for that." Randall Kenan certainly seemed to be worrying about this when he asked himself, "Did I, in my attempts to learn and to experience another world, somehow lose, divest, mitigate or disavow who or what I was? Did I, in mingling and commingling with white folks, dilute or pollute or weaken my legacy as a son of a son of a son of slaves stolen from Africa?"[26]

In reality, Kenan's feelings for his African ancestral origins seem ambivalent at best. As he traveled across the nation gathering material for his book on African American identity and attitudes at the millennium, his encounters with black people, in locales as far flung as Utah and Alaska, who yearned for a South they had never seen or experienced made him realize that "[m]ost African-Americans in this country can't trace their roots back to Africa, but they can certainly trace them back to Tennessee, Georgia, North Carolina, Mississippi, the Southern states."[27]

Ralph Ellison had made this point many years earlier when he asserted that his homeland consisted of Abbeville, South Carolina, and Oklahoma City, noting "that is enough for me" and warning that "by raising the possibility of Africa as a 'homeland' we give Africa an importance on the symbolic level that it does not have in the actual thinking of people." Needless to say, no one did more to boost the symbolic importance of an African homeland than Alex Haley, who, as the author of *Roots*, won fortune and acclaim by tracing his own family's historical and cultural ties to Africa. Yet Haley's tendency to wax vividly nostalgic about his small-town

Tennessee boyhood, and his admission that "I don't know anything I treasure more as a writer than being a Southerner," suggests a primary identity more southern than African.[28]

Some black intellectuals actually seemed to think that the South represented both a North American homeland and a cultural way station where blacks could best explore or at least *feel* their connections with Africa without experiencing it first hand. For example, emotional, even spiritual, attachments to place have long been seen as integral elements of both African and southern culture, and John Oliver Killens found it ironic that the Afrocentric apostles of black nationalism in the 1960s and 1970s failed to understand the importance of a southern black experience rooted in "land, earth, soil, dirt. Black dirt: our own black dirt to dig black hands into." Overall, Killens insisted, "the people of the black South are much closer to their African roots, in its culture, its humanity, the beat and rhythms of its music, its concept of family, its dance, and its spirituality." Although she was born in Ohio, Toni Morrison consistently presented the South as a spiritual bridge to Africa and the bedrock not just of black suffering and struggle but of black identity as well. Morrison's characters, Deborah H. Barnes has observed, "recognize the South as . . . the wellspring of their notions of identity, community, [and] nurturance." Several commentators have argued that Morrison's novels warn blacks against "disremembering" their southern roots. Patricia Yeager has suggested that Morrison and other African American women writers who were not born in the South nonetheless "needed to think about the South as a way to think about the meaning of being black and . . . needed to think about the meaning of being black as a way of thinking about the South."[29]

Though he too was born and raised elsewhere, Eddy Harris echoed Randall Kenan when he reflected on his first visit to the South: "I did not travel across Africa to find my roots. I traveled South to find them. For the South, not Africa, is home to Black Americans and Black Americans as a race are essentially southerners. Only in the South could I discover where my beginnings as a Black American have gone. Without realizing it at the time, I was going home." Harris understood that he had "found my roots," that his journey to "touch the soul of the South" actually led him to the discovery of "my own black soul."[30]

Even for those who tried, separating the sources and symbols of their southernness from those of their blackness was no easy matter. Though he did not object to being seen as a southern writer, Randall Kenan sometimes wondered whether "I am a writer of the South and about the South or a writer of blackness." In his early years blackness had meant "a pointillism of culture" that included "collard greens. 'Amazing Grace, How Sweet the Sound.' . . . head rags and chitlins, 'Chain of Fools' and 'Swing Low Sweet Chariot.' Ultra-sheen, Afro-sheen, neck bones, [and] cornrows." It is noteworthy that many of what Kenan called "these signs and symbols" that were "the air I breathed, the water I drank, the ground upon which I walked" were also the signifiers of southernness for many whites as well as African Americans.[31]

When he heard his elderly kin tell stories of the many hardships and scattered joys of "'the old days'" in the South, Kenan had "taken for granted that this tapestry, this ever-reaching-back fabric was what being black was all about." As an adult, however, he seemed to realize that the same figures from his family, school, and church experiences who taught him "those things that I had taken so for granted about being black" had also shaped his ideas about being southern. Surveying the contemporary scene, Kenan worried that the experiences of black children in his tiny North Carolina hometown are now little different from those of black children anywhere in the nation, and he realized that "[w]hat's true of African American identity is true for southern identity. A lot of it is fragile and in danger, and a lot of it is so much a part of us that we don't even see it."[32]

Although the events of the last half of the twentieth century made the Jim Crow system that had stood between African Americans and their identity as southerners a thing of the past, when it comes to identities, things of the past often overshadow things of the present. This is readily apparent in the ongoing conflicts over the Confederate flag and other historical symbols linked by many to white racial oppression, as well as in the efforts of African Americans to construct monuments and memorials to their struggle to free the South from the racial system constructed from the rubble of the Confederate legacy.

It is tempting to buy into well-intentioned suggestions that in constructing a common future, black and white southerners can draw on a common past. At the very least, however, theirs is a common past both experienced and perceived quite differently. After all, slavery meant poverty and suffering for blacks and wealth and ease for the whites who owned them, while emancipation was an emotional triumph for blacks and an economic disaster for many whites. Likewise, Reconstruction was generally a time of hope for blacks and a bummer for whites. An editorial writer for the *Greensboro News and Record* was quite likely correct when he concluded, "It's unlikely in our lifetimes or the lifetimes of our children that the South will become the kind of melting pot that allows all its citizens to adopt a common view of its racial past."[33]

Efforts to control the representation of the past involve more than the mere pursuit of an abstract sense of emotional gratification. As Jacques Le Goff explained, those "who have dominated and continue to dominate" have long sought "to make themselves the masters of memory and forgetfulness." In 1982 I was a member of the University of Mississippi's faculty Senate, which approved unanimously a resolution urging that the university disassociate itself from the Confederate flag. In the wake of that vote I penned an opinion piece suggesting that historical symbols like the Confederate flag are often contested because, by virtue of the way they link the present to the past, they reveal "who still rules, who still gives, who still gets and whose preferences are still respected." Thus the real issue in conflicts like the one over the Rebel flag was "not tradition but power, the power to preserve elements of Mississippi's heritage that are materially and psychologically satisfying to some but may be discouraging and offensive to others."[34]

Shocked by the ubiquitous Confederate imagery that assaulted him on his first visit to the South, Eddy Harris mused, "Symbols are indivisible. . . . If it's mine, it can't be yours." Bitter and frustrated, he demanded of a white southerner, "How do you expect a black person to feel . . . in a society that so blatantly reminds him how emotionally tied his government still is to a system that fought to keep his ancestors in slavery?" As Harris saw it, the white southerners who supported the Confederate flag seemed to be saying: "We don't care if our symbols are hateful to you and upset you or remind you of our inhuman treatment toward you. We don't care because these are sources of our pride and we do not concern ourselves with your pride. These are our symbols and not yours. And you do not share in what is ours."[35]

Harris's reaction underscores the importance of representations of an affirmative black past to making the South seem more comfortable and hospitable to African Americans. As a young girl in early twentieth-century North Carolina, Pauli Murray was already cynical about the meaning of the U.S. flag for black people in the South, but she nonetheless found special comfort each year on Decoration Day or Memorial Day in placing it on the grave of her grandfather, a Union veteran. To Murray, installing "this solitary American flag just outside the iron fence that separated it from the Confederate banners waving on the other side was an act of hunger and defiance. It tied me and my family to something bigger than the Rebel atmosphere in which we found ourselves. . . . [A]nd it helped to negate in my mind the symbols of inferiority and apartness."[36]

Many years later, the Eddy Harris who had been so angered and repulsed by the Confederate symbolism he had encountered upon entering the South had also come to the region shamed and disappointed that his ancestors had not rebelled openly against their enslavement. However, after discovering his great-great grandfather's manumission papers, he finally appreciated what his forebears had endured and overcome, and as he rode out of Richmond, he found that "along Monument Avenue the statues of Lee and Stuart and Jefferson Davis do not seem so chilly as before, not so frightening in their symbolism, for now I have a symbol of my own."[37]

There is no doubt that erecting memorials to the African American freedom struggle and removing the Confederate flag and other "offensive historical monuments" has created what Fitzhugh Brundage calls "a less alienating" public landscape for black southerners. The positive effect of such victories should not be minimized. On the other hand, neither should it be exaggerated. For example, the always divisive politics of the past often seems to derail contemporary progress toward greater interracial cooperation and understanding. A case in point is Selma, Alabama, where the city's first black mayor, James Perkins Jr., found his efforts to break down racial barriers in this old civil rights battleground undermined almost immediately by an emotional conflict over placing a monument to controversial Confederate general Nathan Bedford Forrest on city property.[38]

Elsewhere, Brundage is clearly correct in observing that "groups routinely sort the past in a particular way to legitimize their current power or aspirations," but given the growing disparities in power and the likelihood of concomitant differences in aspirations among African Americans, we should not presume that all members of a group view these disagreements about historical symbols from the same perspective or with the same sense of urgency. For example, politicizing such symbols may not always serve the primary interests of lower-income black southerners for whom other, more pressing and substantive day-to-day needs clearly take precedence over concerns about Confederate flags or civil rights memorials. Berndt

Ostendorf's assertion that "[c]ultural identity . . . is the privilege of the socially secure" may be a little extreme, but there is no question that expressions of concern with symbolic identity intensify as socioeconomic status rises. On the other hand, as historian Dan Carter has pointed out, "Symbols never fed children . . . you can be obsessed in the struggle over symbolic issues as a way of avoiding hard issues." On the eve of a 2001 referendum on removing the Confederate insignia from his state's flag, a black Mississippian explained, "It don't bother me either way it goes. . . . Money's my problem. As far as the flag and that kind of s——, I don't care. I can't live off a flag."[39]

In the midst of a severe fiscal crisis in March 2003, as Georgians watched their legislature spend an entire session arguing about the appearance of the state flag, nearly 70 percent of those polled thought the debate was either a negative or divisive influence or simply a waste of time. Even a self-described "born-and-bred Georgia Rebel," eighty-year-old Frank Hyde, worried about "dividing the races" and pointed to Georgia's need for better roads, schools, and teachers. Veteran civil rights activist and former Atlanta mayor Andrew Young had announced in 2001 that he didn't "give a damn" about the state flag and urged lawmakers to concentrate on more fundamental policy concerns. On the eve of the state's 2004 referendum, Young ignored a compromise flag's ties to the Confederacy and urged Georgians to vote for it in order to "put the flag issue to rest."[40]

Whether the myth-encrusted memorials to the Lost Cause can ever coexist peacefully with the proliferating shrines to the vindicated, if not totally fulfilled, cause of civil rights is impossible to predict, but we can only hope that southerners will at some point realize that such starkly contrasting symbolic juxtapositions are inevitable in a society whose people have encountered history in very different ways and now view it from very different perspectives. In the meantime, by continuing to devote so much of their passion and energy to squabbling over the icons of a past that is so clearly problematic for cooperative future-building, leaders of both races may be jeopardizing their opportunity to build on the *Brown* decision's legacy by constructing not just a new southern identity but a new southern reality, where everyone would be visible and no one's belonging would be denied.

Notes

CHAPTER 1 Stranger Than We Thought

1. J. Milton Yinger and George E. Simpson, "Can Segregation Survive in an Industrial Society?" *Antioch Review* 18 (March 1958), 16; William H. Nicholls, *Southern Tradition and Regional Progress* (Chapel Hill: University of North Carolina Press, 1962), 130.

2. Nicholls, *Southern Tradition*, 181; *Brown v. Board of Education*, 347 U.S. 483 (1954).

3. *Webster's Unabridged Dictionary of the English Language* (New York: Portland House, 1989), 551; C. Vann Woodward, *The Strange Career of Jim Crow* (New York: Oxford University Press, 1955), 88; *Plessy v. Ferguson*, 163 U.S. 537 (1896).

4. *New York Times*, May 18, 1954; *Cavalier Daily*, University of Virginia, May 18, 1954.

5. Woodward, *Strange Career*, ix; C. Vann Woodward, *Thinking Back: The Perils of Writing History* (Baton Rouge: Louisiana State University Press, 1984), 83, 87.

6. Barrington Moore Jr., *Social Origins of Dictatorship and Democracy: Lord and Peasant in the Making of the Modern World* (Boston: Beacon, 1967), 486.

7. C. Vann Woodward, *The Strange Career of Jim Crow*, 2nd rev. ed. (New York: Oxford University Press, 1966), 164.

8. C. Vann Woodward, "Segregation in Historical Perspective," Box 73, Folder 130, Unpublished Papers, 1960–73, C. Vann Woodward Papers, Yale University Manuscripts and Archives, New Haven, Conn.

9. C. Vann Woodward, "Young Jim Crow," *Nation*, July 7, 1956, 9–10.

10. John W. Cell, *The Highest Stage of White Supremacy: The Origins of Segregation in South Africa and the American South* (Cambridge: Cambridge University Press, 1982), 90; Woodward, "Young Jim Crow," 10.

11. Richard Kluger, *Simple Justice: The History of* Brown v. Board of Education *and Black America's Struggle for Equality* (New York: Vintage, 1977),

646; C. Vann Woodward, *Origins of the New South* (Baton Rouge: Louisiana State University Press, 1951), 211–12.

12. Richard H. King, *A Southern Renaissance: The Cultural Awakening of the American South, 1930–1955* (New York: Oxford University Press, 1980), 271; Woodward, *Thinking Back*, 92.

13. Woodward, *Origins*, 211; George Washington Cable, *The Silent South* (New York: Charles Scribner's Sons, 1889).

14. Woodward, *Thinking Back*, 93; Rayford W. Logan, review of *The Strange Career of Jim Crow*, by C. Vann Woodward, *American Historical Review* 61 (1955), 212; E. Franklin Frazier, review of *The Strange Career of Jim Crow*, by C. Vann Woodward, *Saturday Review* 38 (June 11, 1955), 13. See also Rufus E. Clement, review *The Strange Career of Jim Crow*, by C. Vann Woodward, *Journal of Southern History* 21 (November 1955), 557; Woodward, *Thinking Back*, 92.

15. Woodward, *Strange Career*, viii.

16. David M. Potter, "C. Vann Woodward and the Uses of History," in Don E. Fehrenbacher, ed., *History and American Society: Essays of David M. Potter* (New York: Oxford University Press, 1973), 166, 172.

17. Joel Williamson, *After Slavery: The Negro in South Carolina During Reconstruction, 1861–1877* (Chapel Hill: University of North Carolina Press, 1965), 298, 275.

18. Cell, *Highest Stage*, 92; Michael J. Klarman, *From Jim Crow to Civil Rights: The Supreme Court and the Struggle for Civil Rights* (New York: Oxford University Press, 2004), 18, 51.

19. Howard Rabinowitz, *Race, Ethnicity, and Urbanization: Selected Essays by Howard N. Rabinowitz* (Columbia, Mo.: University of Missouri Press, 1994), 138.

20. Cell, *Highest Stage*, x; Williamson, *After Slavery*, 277.

21. Joel Williamson, *The Crucible of Race: Black-White Relations in the American South Since Emancipation* (New York: Oxford University Press, 1984), 253.

22. Ibid., 419.

23. Cell, *Highest Stage*, x; Edward L. Ayers, *The Promise of the New South: Life After Reconstruction* (New York: Oxford University Press, 1992), 137.

24. Barbara Young Welke, *Recasting American Liberty: Gender, Race, Law, and the Railroad Revolution, 1865–1920* (Cambridge: Cambridge University Press, 2001), 296 n. 51.

25. Jennifer Robock, "The Political Economy of Segregation: The Case of Segregated Streetcars," *Journal of Economic History* 46 (December 1986), 899, 906, 916.

26. Cell, *Highest Stage*, 134–35; Howard Rabinowitz, *Race Relations in the Urban South, 1865–1890* (New York: Oxford University Press, 1978).

27. Williamson, *After Slavery*, 298; Steven Hahn, *A Nation Under Our Feet: Black Political Struggles in the Rural South from Slavery to the Great Migration* (Cambridge, Mass.: Harvard University Press, 2003), 566 n. 6.

28. Robert H. Wiebe, *The Search for Order, 1877–1920* (New York: Harper Collins, 1967); Welke, *Recasting American Liberty*, 352; Ayers, *Promise of the New South*, 142, 145.

29. Howard Rabinowitz, *The First New South, 1865–1920* (Arlington Heights, Ill.: Harlan Davidson, 1992), 120; J. Morgan Kousser, *The Shaping of Southern Politics: Suffrage Restriction and the Establishment of the One-Party South, 1880–1910* (New Haven, Conn.: Yale University Press, 1974).

30. Gavin Wright, *Old South, New South: Resolutions in the Southern Economy Since the Civil War* (New York: Basic Books, 1986), 78–79.

31. *Fifty-Eighth and Fifty-Ninth Annual Reports of the Department of Education to the General Assembly of the State of Georgia for the Biennium Ending June 30, 1930*, 278–79, 306.

32. Gavin Wright, *The Political Economy of the Cotton South: Households, Markets, and Wealth in the Nineteenth-Century* (New York: W. W. Norton, 1978), 160.

33. Cell, *Highest Stage*, 142.

34. Woodward, *Origins*, 144; Paul M. Gaston, *The New South Creed: A Study in Southern Mythmaking* (Baton Rouge: Louisiana State University Press, 1976); Cell, *Highest Stage*, 181.

35. Jonathan M. Wiener, *Social Origins of the New South: Alabama, 1860–1885* (Baton Rouge: Louisiana State University Press, 1978), 213.

36. Grace Elizabeth Hale, *Making Whiteness: The Culture of Segregation in the South, 1890–1940* (New York: Pantheon, 1998), 147, 148.

37. Ibid., 144–45.
38. Ayers, *Promise of the New South*, 145. See U. B. Phillips, "The Central Theme of Southern History," *American Historical Review* 34 (October 1928): 30–43.

CHAPTER 2 Down on *Brown*

1. Michael J. Klarman, "*Brown*, Racial Change, and the Civil Rights Movement," *Virginia Law Review* 80 (1994), 52.
2. Michael J. Klarman, "*Brown* at 50," 12, University of Virginia Law School, Public and Legal Theory Working Paper Series, Year 2004, Paper 5, copy in possession of the author; Derrick Bell, *Silent Covenants: Brown v. Board of Education and the Unfulfilled Hopes for Racial Reform* (New York: Oxford University Press, 2004), 5.
3. Morton Sosna, *In Search of the Silent South: Southern Liberals and the Race Issue* (New York: Columbia University Press, 1977), 205.
4. Michael J. Klarman, *From Jim Crow to Civil Rights: The Supreme Court and the Struggle for Civil Rights* (New York: Oxford University Press, 2004), 174; Frank E. Smith, *Congressman from Mississippi* (New York: Pantheon, 1964), 64.
5. Klarman, "*Brown*, Racial Change," 55–56; Bell, *Silent Covenants*, 133.
6. James C. Cobb, *The Most Southern Place on Earth: The Mississippi Delta and the Roots of Regional Identity* (New York: Oxford University Press, 1992), 204.
7. Bill P. Joyner and John P. Thames, "Mississippi's Efforts at Industrialization: A Critical Analysis," *Mississippi Law Journal* 38 (1967), 476–77.
8. Gerald N. Rosenberg, *Hollow Hope: Can Courts Bring About Social Change?* (Chicago: University of Chicago Press, 1991), 158; Klarman, "*Brown*, Racial Change," 43–44.
9. Herbert P. Northrop and Richard L. Rowan, *Negro Employment in Southern Industry* (Philadelphia: University of Pennsylvania Press, 1970), 9, 1, 19.
10. Klarman, *From Jim Crow to Civil Rights*, 115; Richard E. Lonsdale and Clyde B. Browning, "Rural-Urban Locational Preferences of Southern Manufacturers," *Annals of the American Association of Geographers* 61 (June 1971), 262.

11. Michael J. Klarman, "Why *Brown* Had Such an Impact," *History News Network,* Center for History and News Media, George Mason University, http://hnn.us/articles/4506.html (accessed December 22, 2004); Michael J. Klarman, "Reply: *Brown Versus Board of Education*: Facts and Political Correctness," *Virginia Law Review* 80 (February 1994), 197; Stetson Kennedy, *Jim Crow Guide to the U.S.A.: The Laws, Customs, and Etiquette Governing the Conduct of Nonwhites and Other Minorities as Second-Class Citizens* (London: Lawrence and Wishart, 1959), 158; John Egerton, *Speak Now Against the Day: The Generation Before the Civil Rights Movement in the South* (New York: Alfred A. Knopf, 1994), 397; Stephen G. N. Tuck, *Beyond Atlanta: The Struggle for Racial Equality in Georgia, 1940–1980* (Athens: University of Georgia Press, 2001), 67; *Smith v. Allwright,* 321 U.S. 649 (1944).

12. Michael J. Klarman, "How *Brown* Changed Race Relations: The Backlash Thesis," *Journal of American History* 81 (1994), 89; Egerton, *Speak Now,* 397.

13. Numan V. Bartley, *The New South, 1945–1980* (Baton Rouge: Louisiana State University Press, 1995), 28, 30.

14. Anthony Badger, "The Klarman Thesis: Did the Backlash to *Brown* Change Race Relations?" unpublished paper in the possession of the author.

15. Mark Tushnet, *Taking the Constitution Away from the Courts* (Princeton, N.J.: Princeton University Press, 1999), 136; Klarman, "Reply," 196–197.

16. Bell, *Silent Covenants,* 67; Mary L. Dudziak, *Cold War Civil Rights: Race and Image of American Democracy* (Princeton, N.J.: Princeton University Press, 2000), 13.

17. Bartley, *New South,* 54–55; Klarman, *From Jim Crow to Civil Rights,* 183; Egerton, *Speak Now,* 399; Pete Daniel, *Lost Revolutions: The South in the 1950s* (Chapel Hill: University of North Carolina Press, 2000), 25.

18. Egerton, *Speak Now,* 55; Badger, "The Klarman Thesis."

19. Ralph W. McGill, *The South and the Southerner* (Boston: Little, Brown, 1964), 159; Bartley, *The New South,* 7.

20. Bartley, *New South,* 28, 30; Sosna, *In Search,* 19.

21. Sosna, *In Search,* 205; Kenneth Robert Janken, introduction, and Frederick D. Patterson, "The Negro Wants Full Participation in the

American Democracy," in Rayford W. Logan, ed., *What the Negro Wants* (Notre Dame, Ind.: University of Notre Dame Press, 2001), xix, xx, 265.

22. W. T. Couch, "Publisher's Introduction," xxiii; Janken, introduction, xxiii; Sterling Brown, "Count Us In," all in Logan, ed., *What the Negro Wants*, 323.

23. David L. Cohn, review of *Darkwater*, by W. E. B. Du Bois, *Double Dealer* 1 (June 1921), 255–56; David L. Cohn, "How the South Feels," *Atlantic Monthly* 173 (January 1944), 48–51.

24. William Faulkner, *Intruder in the Dust* (New York: Vintage, 1948), 216; Charles D. Pearcy, *Go Slow Now: Faulkner and the Race Question* (Eugene: University of Oregon Books, 1971), 69–70.

25. Egerton, *Speak Now*, 524; Sosna, *In Search*, 163, 166.

26. Daniel, *Lost Revolutions*, 24; Robert Penn Warren, *Who Speaks for the Negro?* (New York: Random House, 1965), 12, 13.

27. Anne Waldron, *Hodding Carter: The Reconstruction of a Racist* (Chapel Hill: Algonquin, 1993), 248.

28. Hollinger F. Barnard, ed., *Outside the Magic Circle: The Autobiography of Virginia Durr* (Tuscaloosa: University of Alabama Press, 1985), 276; Daniel, *Lost Revolutions*, 32.

29. Pat Watters, *The South and the Nation* (New York: Pantheon, 1969), 286; Pat Watters, *Down to Now: Reflections on the Southern Civil Rights Movement* (New York: Pantheon, 1971), 30.

30. Willie Morris, *North Toward Home* (reprint, Oxford, Miss.: Yoknapatawpha Press, 1982), 140–41.

31. Ibid., 78.

32. Melton A. McLaurin, *Separate Pasts: Growing Up White in the Segregated South* (Athens: University of Georgia Press, 1987), 90; Hortense Powdermaker, *After Freedom: A Cultural Study in the Deep South* (New York: Holiday House, 1968), 301–2, 168.

33. Rosenberg, *Hollow Hope*, 169; Klarman, *From Jim Crow to Civil Rights*, 6, 60, 366.

34. Rosenberg, *Hollow Hope*, 169.

35. David J. Garrow, "Hopelessly Hollow History: Revisionist Devaluing of *Brown v. Board of Education*," *Virginia Law Review* 80 (February 1994), 155.

36. Klarman, "Why *Brown* Had Such an Impact."

37. Ibid.

38. Rosenberg, *Hollow Hope*, 342; Bell, *Silent Covenants*, 23, 24.

39. Raymond Wolters Jr., *The Burden of* Brown: *Thirty Years of School Desegregation* (Knoxville: University of Tennessee Press, 1984), 8. See Tushnet, *Taking the Constitution*, 175.

40. Tushnet, *Taking the Constitution*, 146.

41. Jimmy Buffett, "Permanent Reminder of a Temporary Feeling" (Margaritaville, 1999).

42. Bell, *Silent Covenants*, 4–5; Charles J. Ogletree Jr., *All Deliberate Speed: Reflections on the First Half Century of* Brown v. Board of Education, (New York: W. W. Norton, 2004), 311.

CHAPTER 3 *Brown* and Belonging

1. Sterling Brown, "Count Us In," in Rayford W. Logan, ed., *What the Negro Wants* (Notre Dame, Ind.: University of Notre Dame Press, 2001), 308–9. Portions of this chapter first appeared in "Redefining Southern Culture: Community and Identity," *Georgia Review* 50 (spring 1996), 9–24.

2. Richard Wright, *Black Boy* (New York: Harper and Row, 1966), 284.

3. John F. Callahan, "American Culture Is of a Whole: From the Letters of Ralph Ellison," *New Republic*, March 1, 1999, 38–39.

4. Brown, "Count Us In," 336; Richard Kluger, *Simple Justice: The History of* Brown v. Board of Education *and Black America's Struggle for Equality* (New York: Vintage, 1977), 705; Eric J. Sundquist, "Blues for Atticus Finch: Scottsboro, *Brown*, and Harper Lee," in Larry J. Griffin and Don H. Doyle, eds., *The South as an American Problem* (Athens: University of Georgia Press, 1995), 189.

5. "Transcript of the American Academy Conference on the Negro American, May 14–15, 1965," *Daedalus* (winter 1966), 441.

6. Merle Black and John Shelton Reed, "Blacks and Southerners: A Research Note," *Journal of Politics* 44 (February 1982), 169; Larry J. Griffin and Ashley B. Thompson, "Enough About the Disappearing South: What About the Disappearing Southerner?" *Southern Cultures* 9 (fall 2003), 59.

7. Peter Applebome, "A Sweetness Tempers the South's Bitter Past," *New York Times*, July 31, 1994, pp. 1, 20; Peter Applebome, *Dixie Rising: How the South Is Shaping American Values, Politics, and Culture* (New York: Times Books, 1996), 341; Fred Powledge, *Journeys Through the South: A Rediscovery* (New York: Random House, 1989), 18.

8. Alice Walker, *In Search of Our Mother's Gardens: Womanist Prose* (New York: Harcourt, 1983), 145; Henry Louis Gates Jr., *America Behind the Color Line: Dialogues with African Americans* (New York: Warner Books, 2004), 143.

9. William H. Frey, "Migration to the South Brings Blacks Full Circle," *Population Today*, May–June 2001, www.prb.org (accessed December 23, 2004).

10. Thadious M. Davis, "Expanding the Limits: The Intersection of Race and Region," *Southern Literary Journal* 20 (spring 1988), 6; L. D. Reddick, "The Negro as Southerner and American," in Charles Grier Sellers Jr., ed., *The Southerner as American* (Chapel Hill: University of North Carolina Press, 1960), 130–34; John Hope Franklin, "The South: Perspective for Tomorrow," in *The Future of the South, American Issues Forum I* (Durham, N.C.: Duke University Press, 1994), 7.

11. Thadious M. Davis, "Southern Standard Bearers in the New Negro Renaissance," in Louis D. Rubin Jr. et al., eds., *The History of Southern Literature* (Baton Rouge: Louisiana State University Press, 1985), 291; Richard Wright, *Uncle Tom's Children* (1940; reprint, New York: Harper and Row, 1965), 27, 126.

12. Langston Hughes, "The South," *Crisis* (June 1922), 72; Robert Bone, *Down Home: A History of African American Short Fiction from Its Beginnings to the End of the Harlem Renaissance* (New York: Putnam, 1975), xix–xx; V. Hunt, "A Conversation with Randall Kenan," *African American Review* 29 (autumn 1995), 413.

13. "Transcript of the American Academy Conference," 441; Helen Taylor, *Circling Dixie: Contemporary Southern Culture Through a Transatlantic Lens* (New Brunswick, N.J.: Rutgers University Press, 2001), 173; Walker, *In Search of Our Mother's Gardens*, 20–21.

14. Nikki Giovanni, *Gemini: An Extended Autobiographical Statement on My First Twenty-five Years of Being a Black Poet* (New York: Bobbs-Merrill,

1971), 12; Nikki Giovanni, *Black Feeling, Black Talk, Black Judgment* (New York: William Morrow, 1970), 58; Nikki Giovanni, *Knoxville, Tennessee* (New York: Scholastic Books, 1994).

15. Jack Temple Kirby, *Media-Made Dixie: The South in the American Imagination* (Baton Rouge: Louisiana State University Press, 1978), 183–88.

16. "Randall Kenan Is 1997 Grisham Writer in Residence," *Southern Register*, University of Mississippi (fall 1997), 16; *Charleston News and Courier*, October 20, 1991; Frank Shelton, "Of Machines and Men: Pastoralism in Gaines' Fiction," in David C. Estes, ed., *Critical Reflections on the Fiction of Ernest J. Gaines* (Athens: University of Georgia Press, 1994), 28–29.

17. Fred Hobson, *The Southern Writer and the Post-Modern World*, Mercer University Lamar Memorial Lectures, No. 33 (Athens: University of Georgia Press, 1991), 101.

18. Ibid.; Walker, *In Search of Our Mother's Gardens*, 17.

19. Clifton L. Taulbert, *Once Upon a Time When We Were Colored* (Tulsa, Okla.: Council Oaks Books, 1989), 5–6. See also Onita Estes-Hicks, "The Way We Were: Precious Memories of the Black Segregated South," *African American Review* 27 (spring 1993), 9–17.

20. Belle Gayle Chevigny, "Still It's a Fight for Power," *Nation*, August 22–29, 1994, 196; *New York Times*, July 31, 1994.

21. Barbara Shircliffe, "We Got the Best of That World: A Case for the Study of Nostalgia in the Oral History of School Segregation," *Oral History Review* 28 (summer–fall 2001), 67, 70–71, 77; Henry Louis Gates Jr., *Colored People: A Memoir* (New York: Alfred A. Knopf, 1994), 213.

22. Ray Furlong, "Germans Flock to Nostalgia Film," *BBC News: UK Edition*, March 10, 2003, http://news.bbc.co.uk/1/hi/entertainment/film/2836215.stm (accessed December 23, 2004).

23. Adolph Reed Jr., "Dangerous Dream," *Village Voice*, April 16, 1996, 26, 24; U.S. Census Bureau Historical Income, Table F-3a, Mean Income Received by Each Fifth and Top Five Percent of White Families, 1966 to 2001, http://www.census.gov/hhes/income/histinc/f03a.html (accessed February 9, 2005); Table F-3B, Mean Income Received by Each Fifth and Top 5 Percent of Black Families, 1966–2001, http://www.census.gov/hhes/income/histinc/f03b.html (accessed February 9, 2005).

24. Walker, *In Search of Our Mother's Gardens*, 17; Liane Gay Rozzell, letter to editor, *New Yorker*, March 17, 2003, 18; Belle Gayle Chevigny, "Mississippi Stories I: The Fruits of Freedom Summer," *Nation*, August 8–15, 1994, 157; "Journey to the Center of a Race," interview of Randall Kenan by Fetzer Mills Jr., *Salon*, February 24, 1999, http://archive.salon.com/books/int/1999/02/cov_24int.html (accessed December 23, 2004).

25. "Single Black Female, in Her Own House; Black Home-owners," *Economist.com* (November 20, 2004).

26. Adrian Walker, "Rich Redefine the Struggle," *Boston Globe*, January 19, 2004, p. B1; Randall Kenan, *Walking on Water: Black American Lives at the Turn of the Century* (New York: Little Brown, 1999), 627. See also Gates, *America Behind the Color Line*, passim.

27. Michelle Orecklin, "A Twist on Tradition," *Time*, July 10, 2000, http://www.time.com/time/archive/preview/0,10987,997388,00.html (accessed December 23, 2004).

28. Applebome, *Dixie Rising*, 339; "Transcript of the American Academy Conference," 440.

29. John Oliver Killens, introduction to John Oliver Killens and Jerry W. Ward Jr., eds., *Black Southern Voices: An Anthology of Fiction, Poetry, Drama, Nonfiction, and Critical Essays* (New York: Meridian, 1992), 2–3; Deborah H. Barnes, "Myth, Metaphor, and Memory in Toni Morrison's Reconstructed South," *Studies in the Literary Imagination* 31 (fall 1998), 29; Patricia Yeager, *Dirt and Desire: Reconstructing Southern Women's Writing, 1930–1990* (Chicago: University of Chicago Press, 2000), 56.

30. Eddy L. Harris, *South of Haunted Dreams: A Ride Through Slavery's Back Yard* (New York: Simon and Schuster, 1993), 171, 192–93.

31. Kenan, *Walking on Water*, 7.

32. Ibid., 6–7, 612; Orecklin, "Twist on Tradition."

33. *Greensboro News and Record*, January 20, 1998.

34. W. Fitzhugh Brundage, "No Deed but Memory," in W. Fitzhugh Brundage, ed., *Where These Memories Grow: History, Memory, and Southern Identity* (Chapel Hill: University of North Carolina Press, 2000), 11; James C. Cobb, "Learning to Disagree About the Past," in Clyde V. Williams, ed., *From Behind the Magnolia Curtain: Voices of Mississippi*

(Jackson: Mississippi Press Association/Mississippi Humanities Council, 1988), 6.

35. Harris, *South of Haunted Dreams*, 124–25.

36. Pauli Murray, *Proud Shoes: The Story of an American Family* (New York, Harper and Row, 1978), 275.

37. Harris, *South of Haunted Dreams*, 148.

38. Brundage, "No Deed but Memory," 19; *Financial Times*, May 18, 2001; *Seattle Times*, September 7, 2002.

39. Brundage, "No Deed but Memory," 11; Berndt Ostendorf, *Black Literature in White America* (Sussex, U.K.: Harvester Press, 1982), 128; *The Irish Times*, April 5, 1997; *New Orleans Times-Picayune*, April 16, 2001.

40. *Atlanta Journal-Constitution*, January 21, 2001, March 18, 2003; Georgia Chamber of Commerce, "Put the Focus on the Future . . . Not the Past," mailing flier in possession of the author.

Index

South," 18; on segregation, 18, 27

Graham, Frank Porter, 39

Hahn, Steven, 22

Hale, Grace, 29

Haley, Alex, 68–69

Harlem Renaissance, 61

Harris, Eddy, 69, 72

Hobson, Fred, 63–64

House Un-American Activities Committee (HUAC), 39

Hughes, Langston, 41, 61

Industry, southern: discrimination in, 25–27, 34, 35; and disfranchisement, 28; dispersed pattern of, after World War II, 36; pursuit of, 27–28; and racial change, 35; and segregation, 25, 27, 35

Jim Crow system, 46. *See also* Segregation

Judicial review, 52–53

Kenan, Randall: on loss of black community, 66–68; as southern writer, 63; on southernness and blackness, 70

Killens, John Oliver, 69

King, Rev. Martin Luther, Jr.: on *Brown* decision, 48; as southern black leader, 59; on *Strange Career of Jim Crow*, 13

King, Richard H., 12

Klarman, Michael J.: on black voter

registration in 1940s, 36; as critic of *Brown* decision, 31, 49; on impact of agricultural mechanization, 33; on industrial recruitment and racial progress, 34–35; on NAACP decision to pursue school integration, 36; on origins of segregation, 16; on pre-*Brown* southern racial transformation, 43; on racial progress without *Brown* decision, 50; on Supreme Court and public opinion, 47; on white backlash against *Brown*, 49

Ku Klux Klan, 33

Le Goff, Jacques, 71

Liberals, southern, 40–43

Little Rock, 7, 33

Logan, Rayford W., 13, 41

Long, Earl, 37

Lucy, Autherine, 38, 49

Majette, Denise, 67

Manufacturing. *See* Industry, southern

Massive resistance, 49

McCray, John, 39

McGill, Ralph, 39–40

McKinney, Cynthia, 67

McLaurin, Melton, 47

McMath, Sid, 37

Mechanization in agriculture, 33–34

Mississippi: flag referendum in, 74; resistance in, to black voting, 36